Dogs

A LITERARY ANTHOLOGY

Dogs

A LITERARY ANTHOLOGY

Edited by Catherine Bradley

The British Library

Contents

144 Lost Friends

The Great
Dog Family

———

Dodie Smith (1896–1990)

From *The Hundred and One Dalmatians*

When snow first began to fall, everyone felt worse than ever. 'And Missis didn't even take her coat,' said Mrs. Dearly. She pictured Pongo and Missis lost, shivering and starving. So did Mr. Dearly. But they kept the horrid thought to themselves ...

She went back to the sofa and stroked Perdita who, for once, did no washing but just gazed at the falling snow flakes. The voices singing 'Silent Night' were high and clear and peaceful, and not very loud.

Suddenly, everyone in the room heard a dog bark.

'That's Pongo,' cried Mr. Dearly, and dashed to a window.

'That's Missis,' cried Mrs. Dearly, hearing a different bark as she, too, dashed to a window.

They flung the windows open wide and stared down through the swirling snow. And then their hearts seemed turned to lead by disappointment.

Down below were two black dogs.

Mrs. Dearly said gently: 'You shouldn't be out on a night like this. Go home to your owners, my dears.'

The dogs barked again but Mr. Dearly said 'Home!' very firmly, for he felt sure the dogs lived somewhere near and had been let out for a last run before going to bed. He shut the window, saying to Mrs. Dearly: 'Odd-looking dogs. I can't quite recognise the breed.'

He did not hear the despairing howl that came from Missis. It had happened just as she had feared! They were turned away, outcasts in the night.

Pongo had a moment of panic. This was something he had not foreseen. But quickly he pulled himself together. 'We must bark again,' he said, 'and much louder.'

. . .

So he barked again, and then Missis barked. They went on and on, taking it in turns.

. . .

'Anyone would think they knew us,' said Mr. Dearly. 'I shall go down and see if they have collars on. Perhaps I can take them to their homes.'

Pongo heard this and said to Missis quickly: 'The moment the door opens, dash in and lead the way up to the drawing-room. Pups, you follow Missis, nose to tails. I will bring up the rear. And never let there be one moment when Mr. Dearly can close the front door. Once we are in, we can make them understand.'

The front door opened and out came Mr. Dearly. In shot Missis, closely followed by the Cadpig – now out of her cart – and all her brothers and sisters except Lucky, who insisted on waiting with Pongo. What with the darkness and the whirling snow, Mr. Dearly did not see what was happening until a pup bumped into him in passing (it was Roly Poly – of course). Then he looked down to see what had bumped him and saw a steady stream of black pups going through the front door and the white hall and up the white stairs.

'I'm dreaming this,' thought Mr. Dearly, and pinched himself, hard. But the stream of pups went on and on.

Suddenly there was a hitch. The two pups faithfully dragging the Cadpig's little blue cart, now empty, could not get it up the steps. Mr. Dearly, who could never see a dog in difficulty without helping, at once picked the cart up himself. After seeing the cart, he no longer felt he was dreaming. 'These dogs are a troop from a circus,' he thought. 'But why have they come to us?'

A moment later, Pongo and Lucky went past and the stream of dogs stopped. Mr. Dearly called into the night: 'Any more out there?' To his relief no dog answered, so he went in and closed the door. Pongo's sooty hindquarters were just rounding a bend of the stairs. Mr. Dearly followed four steps at a time, still carrying the little blue cart.

The scene in the front drawing-room was rather confused. Large as the room was, there was not floor space for all the puppies, so they were jumping on to tables and chairs and piling up on top of each other. There was rather a lot of noise. Mrs. Dearly was just managing to keep on her feet. She had never been frightened of any dog in her life, but she did feel a trifle startled. The Nannies had taken refuge on top of the grand piano.

Mr. Dearly took one look through the door, then dashed into the back drawing-room and flung open the double doors. A sea of pups surged in. And now that there was a little spare floor space, Pongo barked a command:

'All pups who can find space: Roll! Roll, Missis!' And he himself rolled with a will.

The Dearlys stared in utter bewilderment – and then both of them shouted: 'Look!'

The white carpet was becoming blacker, the black dogs were becoming whiter –

'It's Pongo!' cried Mr. Dearly.

'It's Missis!' cried Mrs. Dearly.

'It's Pongo, Missis and all their puppies!' cried the Nannies from the top of the piano.

'It's considerably more than all their puppies,' said Mr. Dearly – just before Pongo forcibly embraced him.

Eleanor Farjeon (1881–1965)

Dog

Whether I'm Alsatian,
  Dachshund or Dalmatian,
Or any one among the Terrier crew,
  However brief you've known me,
  As long as you will own me,
I'm Dog, that's all, my Master, Dog to you.

If you like a Setter
  Or a Spaniel better,
Aberdeen or Airedale – some folk do –
  Whatever breed you name me,
  As long as you will claim me
I'm yours for life, my Master, Dog to you.

I'll love you, Cairn or Collie,
  Beyond the point of folly,
And if I'm Mongrel, love you just as true;
  Kick me or caress me,
  As long as you possess me
I'm yours till death, my Master, Dog to you.

For you, I'll be so knowing!
  I'll whimper at your going,
And at your coming, wag myself in two!
  Trust you while I tease you,
  Pester you to please you,
Your Dog, that's all, my Master, Dog to you.

E.V. Lucas (1868–1938)

The Pekinese

The Pekinese
Adore their ease
    And slumber like the dead;
In comfort curled
They view the world
    As one unending bed.

Edward, Duke of York (early fifteenth century)

Mayster of Game

OF SPANIELS

A good spaniel should not be too rough, but his tail should be rough. The good qualities that such hounds have are these: they love well their masters and follow them without losing, although they be in a great crowd of men, and commonly they go before their master, running and wagging the tail, and raise or start fowl or wild beasts. But their right craft is of the partridge and of the quail. It is a good thing to a man that hath a noble goshawk or a tiercel or a sparrow hawk for partridge, to have such hounds. And also when they be taught to be couchers, they be good to take partridges and quail with a net. And also they be good when they are taught to swim and to be good for the river, and for fowls when they have dived ... Hounds for the hawk are fighters and great barkers if you lead them a hunting among running hounds, whatever beasts they hunt to they will make them lose the line, for they will go before now hither now thither, as much when they are at fault as when they go right, and lead the hounds about and make them overshoot and fail. Also if you lead greyhounds with you, and there be a hound for the hawk, that is to say a spaniel, if he see geese or kine, or horses, or hens, or oxen or other beasts, he will run anon and begin to bark at them, and because of him all the greyhounds will run to take the beast through his egging on, for he will make all the riot and all the harm.

William Shakespeare (1564–1616)

From *Macbeth*

Ay, in the catalogue ye go for men,
As hounds and grey-hounds, mongrels, spaniels, curs
Shoughs, water rugs, and demi-wolves are clept
All by the name of dogs: the valu'd file
Distinguishes the swift, the slow, the subtle,
The house-keeper, the hunter, every one
According to the gift which bounteous Nature
Hath in him clos'd; whereby he does receive
Particular addition, from the bill
That writes them all alike: and so of men.

John Gay (1685–1732)

The Pointer

The subtle dog scours with sagacious nose
Along the field, and snuffs each breeze that blows;
Against the wind he takes his prudent way,
While the strong gale directs him to the prey.
Now the warm scent assures the covey near;
He treads with caution, and he points with fear.
The fluttering coveys from the stubble rise,
And on swift wing divide the sounding skies;
The scattering lead pursues the certain sight.
And death in thunder overtakes their flight.

Dame Juliana Berners (late fifteenth century), from *The Boke of St Albans*

The Properties of a Good Greyhound

A greyhound should be headed like a Snake,
And necked like a Drake,
Footed like a Cat,
Tailed like a Rat,
Sided like a Team,
Chined like a Beam.
The first year he must learn to feed,
The second year to field him lead,
The third year he is fellow-like,

The fourth year there is none sike,
The fifth year he is good enough,
The sixth year he shall hold the plough,
The seventh year he will avail
Great bitches for to assail,
The eighth year lick ladle,
The ninth year cart saddle,
And when he is comen to that year
Have him to the tanner,
For the best hound that ever bitch had
At nine year he is full bad.

R.J. Richardson

The Kerry Blue

The dog from County Kerry
  The tousled tyke and grey,
See how he meets the merry
  And tires them all at play;
Yet, though he's raced and tumbled
  With many a mongrel crew,
The proudest shall be humbled
  That slight the Kerry Blue.

His fathers lived by battle
  Where crags and lakes and bogs
And glens of small black cattle
  Hard work for bold grey dogs;
Shrill Poms he'll scorn with kindness
  Gruff Airedales they shall rue
The day when in their blindness
  They roused the Kerry Blue.

Dark eyes afire for slaughter,
  White teeth to hold and kill
Great otters by the water,
  Big badgers in the hill;
The gamest eighteen-inches
  That ever gripped and slew –
Wise is the foe that flinches
  That flees the Kerry Blue!

Ah, pup that came from Kerry,
    Unfriended and unfed,
To maul my boots and bury
    Your beef-bones in my bed,
You dream of Munster gorses,
    But – here your heart shines through –
You let my tame resources
    Content a Kerry Blue.

Alexander Pope (1688–1744)

Epigram

Engraved on the collar of a dog which
I gave to His Royal Highness

I am his Highness's dog at Kew;
Pray tell me, sir, whose dog are you?

E.V. Lucas (1868–1938)

Black Cocker Spaniels

Of all the dogs that are so sweet,
The spaniel is the most complete;
Of all the spaniels, dearest far
The loving little Cockers are.

They're always merry, always hale;
Their eyes are like October ale;
They are so loyal and so black;
So unresentful 'neath the whack;

They never sulk, they never tire;
They love the field, they love the fire;
They never criticise their friends;
Their every joy all joy transcends.

The Aberdeen is quaint and sly,
A harvest of the anxious eye;
The Bedlington is blue and true;
The Airedale fights till death for you;

The Bob-tail is a jolly chap;
The Pekinese commands your lap;
The Dachshund (with the Queen Anne legs)
Your sympathy enchains or begs.

Yet why compare? All dogs on earth
Possess some special charm and worth.
But Cocker spaniels? Every way,
They are the kennel's angels, they.

William Cowper (1731–1800), from *The Task*

The Lurcher

Forth goes the woodman, leaving unconcerned
The cheerful haunts of men to wield the axe
And drive the wedge in yonder forest drear,
From morn to eve his solitary task.
Shaggy and lean and shrewd, with pointed ears
And tail cropped short, half-lurcher and half-cur,
His dog attends him. Close behind his heel
Now creeps he slow, and now with many a frisk
Wide scampering, snatches up the drifted snow
With ivory teeth, or ploughs it with his snout;
Then shakes his powder'd coat, and barks for joy.

Dorothy Margaret Stuart (1889–1963)

King George's Dalmatian AD 1822

Yellow wheels and red wheels, wheels that squeak and roar,
Big buttons, brown wigs, and many capes of buff ...
Someone's bound for Sussex in a coach-and-four;
And when the long whips crack,
Running at the back
Barks the swift Dalmatian
Whose spots are seven score.

White dust and grey dust, fleeting tree and tower,
Brass horns and copper horns blowing loud and bluff,
Someone's bound for Sussex at eleven miles an hour;
And, when the long horns blow,
From the dust below
Barks the swift Dalmatian,
Tongued like an apple flower.

Big domes and little domes, donkey-carts that jog,
High stocks and low pumps and incomparable snuff,
Someone strolls at Brighton, not very much incog.;
And, panting on the grass,
In his collar bossed with brass,
Lies the swift Dalmatian,
The King's plum-pudding dog.

Edward, Duke of York (early fifteenth century)

Mayster of Game

OF GREYHOUNDS AND THEIR NATURE
The good greyhound should be of middle size, neither too big nor
too little, and then he is good for all beasts. If he were too big he is
nought for small beasts, and if he were too little he were nought for
the great beasts. Nevertheless whoso can maintain both, it is good
that he have both of the great and of the small, and of the middle
size. A greyhound should have a long head and somewhat large made,
resembling the making of a bace [pike]. A good large mouth and
good seizers the one against the other, so that the nether jaw pass not

the upper, nor that the upper pass not the nether. Their eyes are red or black as those of a sparrow hawk, the ears small and high in the manner of a serpent, the neck great and long bowed like a swan's neck, his chest great and open, the hair under his chyn hanging down in the manner of a lion. His shoulders as a roebuck, the forelegs straight and round as a cat, great claws, long head as a cow hanging down.

The bones and the joints of the chine great and hard like the chine of a hart. And if his chine be a little high it is better than if it were flat. A little pintel and little ballocks, and well trussed near the ars, small womb and straight near the back as a lamprey, the thighs great and straight as a hare, the hocks straight and not bent as of an ox, a cat's tail making a ring at the end and not too high, the two bones of the chine behind broad of a large palm's breadth or more. Also there are many good greyhounds with long tails right swift. A good greyhound should go so fast that if he be well slipped he should overtake any beast, and there where he overtakes it he should seize it where he can get at it the soonest, nevertheless he shall last longer if he bite in front or by the side. He should be courteous and not too fierce, following well his master and doing whatever he command him. He shall be good and kindly and clean, glad and joyful and playful, well willing and goodly to all manner of folks save to the wild beasts to whom he should be fierce, spiteful and eager.

William Shakespeare (1582–1616)

From *A Midsummer Night's Dream*

My hounds are bred out of the Spartan kind,
So flew'd, so sanded; and their heads are hung
With ears that sweep away the morning dew,
Crook knee'd, and dew-lapped like Thessalian bulls;
Slow in pursuit, but matched in mouth like bells,
Each under each. A cry more tuneable
Wasnever holla'd to, nor cheer'd with horn,
In Crete, in Sparta, nor in Thessaly:
Judge, when you hear.

Geoffrey Chaucer (1343–1400)

From *The Book of the Duchess*

I was go walked fro my tree,
And as I wente, ther came by mee
A whelp, that fauned me as I stood,
That hadde yfolowed, and koude no good.
Hyt com and crepte to me as lowe
Ryght as hyt hadde me yknowe,
Helde doun hys hed and joined hys eres,
And leyde al smothe doun hys heres.
I wolde have kaught hyt, and anoon
Hyt fledde, and was fro me goon;
And hym I folwed, and hyt forth wente
Doun by a floury grene wente.

F. Conquest

A Stern Story

I have a little puppy, and he often runs around
    And tries to catch the tail he hasn't got;
He always seems surprised and hurt to see it can't be found,
    But knowing men assure me he is not.
Because he was so little that his baby eyes were shut,
    He never saw it so he never knew
How very nice and long it was before they had it cut,
    And only left him just an inch or two.

Dachshund 1.

87

Dachshund

91

They say he looks more handsome and is saved a lot of woes;
    One can't step on a tail that is no more;
Hot cinders cannot burn it, and as every Manx cat knows,
    It can't get caught within a slamming door.
But he quivers with excitement from his head down to his toes
    When I light back from the station with my bag,
And he wriggles from his little stump right to his little nose,
    And I know he'd like a longer tail to wag.

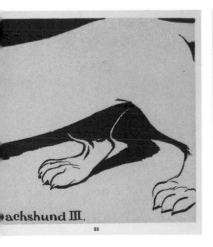

achshund III.

Dachshund IV.

Dogs at Work
and Play

Julian Grenfell (1888–1915)

To a Black Greyhound

Shining black in the shining light,
   Inky black in the golden sun,
Graceful as the swallow's flight,
   Light as a swallow, winged one,
Swift as driven hurricane –
   Double-sinewed stretch and spring,
Muffled thud of flying feet,
   See the black dog galloping,
   Hear his wild foot-beat.

See him when the day is dead,
   Black curves curled on the boarded floor.
Sleepy eyes, my sleepy-head –
   Eyes that were aflame before.
Gentle now, they burn no more;
   Gentle now and softly warm,
With the fire that made them bright
   Hidden – as when after storm
   Softly falls the night.

God of speed, who makes the fire –
   God of Peace, who lulls the same –
God who gives the fierce desire,
   Lust for blood as fierce as flame –
God who stands in Pity's name –
   Many may ye be or less,

Ye who rule the earth and sun:
  Gods of strength and gentleness,
  Ye are ever one.

William Wordsworth (1770–1850)

Incident Characteristic of a Favourite Dog

On his morning rounds the master
Goes to learn how all things fare;
Searches pasture after pasture,
Sheep and cattle eyes with care;
And for silence, or for talk,
He hath comrades in his walk;
Four dogs each pair of a different breed,
Distinguished, two for scent, and two for speed.

See a hare before him started!
  – Off they fly in earnest chase;
Every dog is eager-hearted,
All the four are in the race!
And the hare whom they pursue
Knows from instinct what to do;
Her hope is near; no turn she makes;
But like an arrow to the river takes.

Deep the river was and crusted
Thinly by a one night's frost;

But the nimble hare hath trusted
To the ice, and safely crost;
She hath crost, and without heed
All are following at full speed,
When lo! the ice so thinly spread,
Breaks, and the greyhound Dart is overhead!

Better fate have Prince and Swallow –
See them cleaving to the sport!
Music has no heart to follow,
Little Music, she stops short.
She hath neither wish nor heart,
Hers is now another part:
A lovely creature she, and brave!
And fondly strives her struggling friend to save.

From the brink her paws she stretches,
Very hands as you would say!
And afflicting moans she fetches,
As he breaks the ice away.
For herself she hath no fears, –
Him alone she sees and hears, –
Makes efforts with complainings; nor gives o'er
Until her fellow sinks to reappear no more.

Patrick Chalmers (1872–1942)

Fan

Fan, the hunt terrier, runs with the pack,
A little white bitch with a patch on her back;
She runs with the pack as her ancestors ran –
We've an old-fashioned lot here, and breed 'em like Fan;
Round of skull, harsh of coat, game and little and low,
The sort that we bred sixty seasons ago.

So she's harder than nails, and she's nothing to learn
From her scarred little snout to her cropped little stern,
And she hops along gaily, in spite of her size,
With twenty-four couple of big badger-pyes.
('Tis slow, but 'tis sure is the old white and grey,
And 'twill sing to a fox for a whole winter day.)
Last year at Rook's Rough, just as Ben put 'em in
'Twas Fan found the rogue who was curled in the whin;
She pounced at his brush with a dive and a snap,
'Yip-Yap, boys,' she told 'em, 'I've found him, Yip-Yap!'
And they put down their noses and spoke to his line
Like bells in a steeple most stately and fine.

'Twas a point of ten miles and a kill in the dark
That frightened the pheasants in Fallowfield Park,
And into the worry flew Fan like a shot
And snatched the tit-bit that old Rummage had got;
Eloop, little Fan with the patch on her back,
She broke up her fox with the best of the pack.

William Cowper (1731–1800)

On a Spaniel called Beau, Killing a Young Bird, July 15, 1793

A spaniel, Beau, that fares like you,
  Well-fed and at his ease,
Should wiser be than to pursue
  Each trifle that he sees.

But you have killed a tiny bird,
  Which flew not till to-day,
Against my orders, when you heard
  Forbidding you to prey.

Nor did you kill that you might eat
    And ease a doggish pain,
For him, though chased with furious heat,
    You left where he was slain.

Nor was he of the thievish sort,
    Or one whom blood allures,
But innocent was all his sport
    Whom you have torn for yours.

My dog! what remedy remains,
    Since, teach you all I can,
I see you, after all my pains,
    So much resemble man!

William Cowper (1731–1800)

Beau's Reply

Sir, when I flew to seize the bird
    In spite of your command,
A louder voice than yours I heard,
    And harder to withstand.

You cried – forbear! – but in my heart
    A mightier cry – proceed! –
'Twas nature, sir, whose strong behest
    Impelled me to the deed.

Yet much as nature I respect
    I ventured once to break
(As you perhaps may recollect)
    Her precept for your sake;

And when a linnet on a day,
    Passing his prison door,
Had flutter'd all his strength away
    And panting press'd the floor:

Well knowing him a sacred thing,
    Nor destined to my tooth,
I only kiss'd his ruffled wing,
    And licked his feathers smooth.

Let my obedience then excuse
    My disobedience now,
Nor some reproof yourself refuse
    From your aggrieved bow-wow;

If killing birds be such a crime
    (Which I can hardly see,)
What think you, sir, of killing time
    With verse addressed to me?

Walter Emanuel (1869–1915)

From *A Dog Day*

1.25 Upstairs into dining room. Family not finished lunch yet. Young Mr. Brown throws bread pellet at me, hitting me on the nozzle. An insult. I swallow the insult. Then I go up to Miss Brown and look at her with my great pleading eyes. I guessed it: they are irresistible. She gives me a piece of pudding. Aunt Brown tells me she shouldn't. At which, with great pluck, Miss Brown tells her to mind her own business. I admire that girl more and more.

1.30 A windfall. A whole dish of mayonnaise fish on the slab in the hall. Before you can say Jack Robinson I have bolted it.

1.32 Curious pains in my underneath.

1.33 Pains in my underneath get worse.

1.34 Horrid feeling of sickness.

1.35 Rush up into Aunt Brown's room and am sick there.

1.37 Better. Think I shall pull through if I am careful.

Patrick Chalmers (1872–1942)

Patsy

Puppy dog, rough as a bramble,
   Eyed like a saint,
Beggar to slobber and gambol,
   Corky and quaint,
Chasing your tail like a fubsy turbillion,
Plaguing a playmate with fuss of a million

Gnats,
But keen as a kestrel
    And fierce as a stoat is,
A-thrill to ancestral
    Furies at notice
Of rats,
Rats, little hound of Beelzebub, rats!

And as you sleep off a surfeit,
    Mischief and tea.
Prone on the summer-warm turf, it
    Surely must be
(Rapturous whimper and tremulant twitching)
Somewhere or other there's hunting bewitching:
That's
More blessed than biscuit;
    I'll lay, through your slumbers,
They squeak and they frisk it
    In shadowy numbers,
R-r-rats,
Rats, little hound of
Beelzebub, rats!

Virginia Woolf (1882–1941)

From *Flush: A Biography*

And just as Mrs. Browning was exploring her new freedom and
delighting in the discoveries she made, so Flush too was making
his discoveries and exploring his freedom. Before they left Pisa – in
the spring of 1847 they moved on to Florence – Flush had faced
the curious and at first upsetting fact that the laws of the Kennel
Club are not universal. He had brought himself to face the fact
that light topknots are not necessarily fatal. He had revised his
code accordingly. He had acted, at first with some hesitation,
upon his new conception of canine society. He was becoming
daily more and more democratic. Even in Pisa, Mrs. Browning
noticed, '… he goes out every day and speaks Italian to the little
dogs'. Now in Florence the last threads of his old fetters fell from
him. The moment of liberation came one day in the Cascine. As
he raced over the grass 'like emeralds' with 'the pheasants all alive
and flying', Flush suddenly bethought him of Regent's Park and
its proclamation: Dogs must be led on chains. Where was 'must'
now? Where were chains now? Where were park-keepers and
truncheons? Gone, with the dog-stealers and Kennel Clubs and
Spaniel Clubs of a corrupt aristocracy! Gone with four-wheelers
and hansom cabs! with Whitehall and Shoreditch! He ran; he
raced; his coat flashed; his eyes blazed. He was the friend of all
the world now. All dogs were his brothers. He had no need of
a chain in this new world: he had no need of protection. If Mr.
Browning was late in going for his walk – he and Flush were the
best of friends now – Flush boldly summoned him. He 'stands
up before him and barks in the most imperious manner possible',
Mrs. Browning observed with some irritation – for her relations

with Flush were far less emotional now than in the old days; she no longer needed his red fur and his bright eyes to give her what her own experience lacked; she had found Pan for herself among the vineyards and the olive trees; he was there too beside the pine fire of an evening. So if Mr. Browning loitered, Flush stood up and barked; but if Mr. Browning preferred to stay at home and write, it did not matter. Flush was independent now. The wistarias and the laburnum were flowering over walls; the judas trees were burning bright in the gardens; the wild tulips were sprinkled in the fields. Why should he wait? Off he ran by himself. He was his own master now. '... he goes out by himself, and stays hours together,' Mrs. Browning wrote; '... knows every street in Florence – will have his own way in everything. I am never frightened at his absence,' she added, remembering with a smile those hours of agony in Wimpole Street and the gang waiting to snatch him up under the horses' feet if she forgot his chain in Vere Street. Fear was unknown in Florence; there were no dog-stealers here and, she may have sighed, there were no fathers.

But, to speak candidly, it was not to stare at pictures, to penetrate into dark churches and look up at dim frescoes, that Flush scampered off when the door of Casa Guidi was left open. It was to enjoy something, it was in search of something denied him all these years. Once the hunting horn of Venus had blown its wild music over the Berkshire fields; he had loved Mr. Partridge's dog; she had borne him a child. Now he heard the same voice pealing down the narrow streets of Florence, but more imperiously, more impetuously, after all these years of silence. Now Flush knew what men can never know – love pure, love simple, love entire; love that brings no train of care in its wake; that has no shame, no remorse; that is here, that is gone, as the bee on the flower is here and is gone. To-day the flower is a rose, tomorrow a lily; now it is the wild thistle on the moor, now the pouched and portentous orchid of the conservatory. So variously, so carelessly Flush embraced the spotted spaniel down the alley, and the brindled dog and the yellow dog – it did not matter which. To Flush it was all the same. He followed the horn wherever the horn blew and the wind wafted it. Love was all; love was enough. No one blamed him for his escapades. Mr. Browning merely laughed – 'Quite disgraceful for a respectable dog like him' – when Flush returned very late at night or early the next morning. And Mrs. Browning laughed too, as Flush flung himself down on the bedroom floor and slept soundly upon the arms of the Guidi family inlaid in scagliola.

Charles Dickens (1812–1870)

From *The Pickwick Papers*

'... Dogs, sir?'

'Not just now,' said Mr Winkle.

'Ah! You should keep dogs – fine animals – sagacious creatures – dog of my own once – Pointer – surprising instinct – out shooting one day – entering enclosure – whistled – dog stopped – whistled again – Ponto – no go; stock still – called him – Ponto, Ponto – wouldn't move – dog transfixed – staring at a board – looked up, saw an inscription – 'Gamekeeper has orders to shoot all dogs found in the enclosure' – wouldn't pass it – wonderful dog – valuable dog that – very.'

'Singular circumstance, that,' said Mr Pickwick. 'Will you allow me to make a note of it?'

'Certainly, sir, certainly – hundred more anecdotes of the same animal.'

Loyalty and Love

Eric Knight (1897–1943)

From *Lassie Come Home*

Sam Carraclough had spoken the truth early that year when he told his son Joe that it was a long way from Greenall Bridge in Yorkshire to the Duke of Rudling's place in Scotland. And it is just as many miles coming the other way, a matter of four hundred miles.

But that would be for a man, travelling straight by road or by train. For an animal how far would it be – an animal that must circle and quest at obstacles, wander and err, back-track and sidetrack till it found a way?

A thousand miles it would be – a thousand miles through strange terrain it had never crossed before, with nothing but instinct to tell direction.

Yes, a thousand miles of mountain and dale, of highland and moor, ploughland and path, ravine and river, beck and burn; a thousand miles of tor and brae, of snow and rain and fog and sun; of wire and thistle and thorn and flint and rock to tear the feet – who could expect a dog to win through that?

Yet, if it were almost a miracle, in his heart Joe Carraclough tried to believe in that miracle – that somehow, wonderfully, inexplicably, his dog would be there some day; there, waiting by the school gate. Each day as he came out of school, his eyes would turn to the spot where Lassie had always waited. And each day there was nothing there, and Joe Carraclough would walk home slowly, silently, stolidly, as did the people of his country.

Always, when school ended, Joe tried to prepare himself – told himself not to be disappointed, because there could be no dog there. Thus, through the long weeks, Joe began to teach himself not to believe in the impossible. He had hoped against hope so long that hope began to die.

But if hope can die in a human, it does not die in an animal. As long as it lives, the hope is there and the faith is there. And so, coming across the schoolyard that day, Joe Carraclough would not believe his eyes. He shook his head and blinked, and rubbed his fists in his eyes, for he thought what he was seeing was a dream. There, walking the last few yards to the school gate was – his dog!

He stood, for the coming of the dog was terrible – her walk was a thing that tore at her breath. Her head and her tail were down almost to the pavement. Each footstep forward seemed a separate effort. It was a crawl rather than a walk. But the steps were made, one by one, and at last the animal dropped in her place by the gate and lay still.

The Joe roused himself. Even if it were a dream, he must do something. In dreams one must try.

He raced across the yard and fell to his knees, and then, when his hands were touching and feeling fur, he knew it was reality. His dog had come to meet him!

But what a dog was this – no prize collie with fine tricolour coat glowing, with ears lifted gladly over the proud, slim head with its perfect black mask. It was not a dog whose bright eyes were alert, and who jumped up to bark a glad welcome. This was a dog that lay, weakly trying to lift a head that would no longer lift; trying to move a tail that was torn and matted with thorns and burrs, and managing to do nothing very much except to whine in a weak, happy, crying way. For she knew that at last the terrible driving instinct was at peace. She was at the place. She had kept her lifelong rendezvous, and hands were touching her that had not touched her for so long a time.

By the Labour Exchange Ian Cawper stood with the other out-of-work miners, waiting till it was tea time so that they could all go back to their cottages.

You could have picked out Ian, for he was much the biggest man, even among the many big men that Yorkshire grows. In fact, he was reputed to be the biggest and strongest man in all that Riding of Yorkshire. A big man, but gentle and often very slow of thinking and speech.

And so Ian was a few seconds behind the others in realizing that something of urgency was happening in the village. Then he saw it too – a boy struggling, half-running, along the main street, his voice lifted in excitement, a great bundle of something in his arms.

The men stirred and moved forward. Then, when the boy was nearer, they heard his cry:

'She's come back! She's come back!'

The men looked at each other and blew out their breath and then stared at the bundle the boy was carrying. It was true. Sam Carraclough's collie had walked back home from Scotland.

'I must get her home, quick!' the boy was saying. He staggered on.

Ian Cawper stepped forward.

'Here,' he said. 'Run on ahead, tell 'em to get ready.'

His great arms cradled the dog – arms that could have carried ten times the weight of this poor, thin animal.

'Oh, hurry, Ian!' the boy cried, dancing in excitement.

'I'm hurrying, lad. Go on ahead.'

So Joe Carraclough raced along the street, turned up the side street, ran down the garden path, and burst into the cottage:

'Mother! Feyther!'

'What is it, lad?'

Joe paused. He could hardly get the words out – the excitement was choking up in his throat, hot and stifling. And then the words were said:

'Lassie! She's come home! Lassie's come home!'

He opened the door, and Ian Cawper, bowing his head to pass under the lintel, carried the dog to the hearth and laid her there.

Jack London (1876–1916)

From *White Fang*

But there was one trial in White Fang's life – Collie. She never gave him a moment's peace. She defied all efforts of the master to make her become friends with White Fang. Ever in his ears was sounding her sharp and nervous snarl. She had never forgiven him the chicken-killing episode, and persistently held to the belief that his intentions were bad. She found him guilty before the act, and treated him accordingly. She became a pest to him, like a policeman following him around the stable and the grounds, and, if he even so much as glanced curiously at a pigeon or chicken, bursting into an outcry of indignation and wrath. His favourite way of ignoring her was to lie down, with his head on his fore-paws, and pretend to sleep. This always dumbfounded and silenced her.

With the exception of Collie, all things went well with White Fang. He had learned control and poise, and he knew the law. He achieved a staidness, and calmness, and philosophical tolerance. He no longer lived in a hostile environment. Danger and hurt and death did not lurk everywhere about him. In time the unknown, as a thing of terror and menace ever impending, faded away. Life was soft and easy. It flowed along smoothly, and neither fear nor foe lurked by the way.

...

White Fang had never been very demonstrative. Beyond his snuggling and the throwing of a crooning note into his love-growl, he had no way of expressing his love. Yet it was given to him to discover a third way. He had always been susceptible to the laughter of the gods. Laughter had affected him with madness, made him frantic with rage. But he did not have it in him to be angry with the love-master, and when that god elected to laugh at him in a good-natured, bantering way, he was nonplussed. He could feel the pricking and stinging of the old anger as it strove to rise up in him, but it strove against love. He could not be angry; yet he had to do something. At first he was dignified, and the master laughed the harder. Then he tried to be more dignified, and the master laughed harder than before. In the end, the master laughed him out of his dignity. His jaws slightly parted, his lips lifted a little, and a quizzical expression that was more love than humour came into his eyes. He had learned to laugh.

Likewise he learned to romp with the master, to be tumbled down and rolled over, and be the victim of innumerable rough tricks. In return he feigned anger, bristling and growling ferociously, and clipping his teeth together that had all the seeming of deadly intention. But he never forgot himself. Those snaps were always delivered on the empty air. At the end of such a romp, when blow and cuff and snap and snarl were fast and furious, they would break off suddenly and stand several feet apart, glaring at each other. And then, just as suddenly, like the sun rising on a stormy sea, they would begin to laugh. This would always culminate with the master's arms going round White Fang's neck and shoulders while the latter crooned and growled his love-song.

But nobody else ever romped with White Fang. He did not permit it. He stood on his dignity, and when they attempted it, his warning snarl and bristling mane were anything but playful. That

he allowed the master these liberties was no reason that he should
be a common dog, loving here and loving there, everybody's
property for a romp and a good time. He loved with single heart
and refused to cheapen himself or his love.

Henry Chappell (1874–1937)

My Little Yorkshire Terrier

Dear little bundle of fluff and fun,
Of silver and shaded tan,
Now looking so solemn and quiet and wise,
Peering out thro' the fringe that lies
In tangled curls o'er the owlish eyes,
That ponder the ways of man.

A tiny terrier of growls and bark,
Teeth in a German set,
That once was a slipper warm and fine,
Tho' guiltless now of shape or shine;
Your foe, dear Vi, was a friend of mine
Ere you and I had met.

Playing and sleeping or chasing poor puss
Make up your little day;
Yet you in your doggie heart are blest
With a virtue rarely by man possessed,
Tho' always claimed and loud professed
By friends of finer clay.

There is Faith in your eyes, my little friend,
Faith – not an empty name;
A lesson for me and the world to learn,
Faith that will never fail or turn
With the veering crowd, but steadfast burn
    A calm and lovely flame.

Elizabeth Barrett Browning (1806–1861)

Flush

But of *Thee* it shall be said,
This dog watched beside a bed
    Day and night unweary,
Watched within a curtained room
Where no sunbeam brake the gloom
    Round the sick and dreary.

Roses, gathered for a vase,
In that chamber died apace,
    Beam and breeze resigning;
This dog only, waited on,
Knowing that, when light is gone
    Love remains for shining.

Jerome K. Jerome (1859–1927)

From *Idle Thoughts of an Idle Fellow*

He looks up at you with his big, true eyes, and says with them,
'Well, you've always got me, you know. We'll go through the world
together, and always stand by each other, won't we?'

He is very imprudent, a dog is. He never makes it his business to
inquire whether you are in the right or the wrong, never bothers as
to whether you are going up or down upon life's ladder, never asks
whether you are rich or poor, silly or wise, sinner or saint. You are

his pal. That is enough for him, and come luck or misfortune, good repute or bad, honour or shame, he is going to stick to you, to comfort you, guard you, give his life for you, if need be – foolish, brainless, soulless dog!

Pliny the Elder (AD 23–79)

From *Natural History*

The domestic animal that is most faithful to man is the dog. Stories are told of the faithfulness of dogs: of a dog that fought robbers that attacked his master ... of a dog in Epirus which recognised his master's murderer in a crowd and pointed him out by barking; of the 200 dogs of the King of Garamantes which escorted him home from exile and fought anyone who got in their way ... Only dogs recognise their master, know when someone is a stranger, recognise their own names and never forget the way to distant places.

Gerald of Wales (twelfth century)

From *The Journey through Wales*

It came to pass also in our days, during the period when the four
sons of Caradoc son of Iestin, and nephews of prince Rhys by his
sister, namely, Morgan, Meredyth, Owen and Cadwallon, bore rule
for their father in those parts, that Cadwallon, through inveterate
malice, slew his brother Owen. But divine vengeance soon
overtook him; for on his making a hostile attack on a certain castle,
he was crushed to pieces by the sudden fall of its walls: and thus,
in the presence of a numerous body of his own and his brother's
forces, suffered the punishment which his barbarous and unnatural
conduct had so justly merited.

Another circumstance which happened here deserves notice. A
greyhound belonging to the aforesaid Owen, large, beautiful, and
curiously spotted with a variety of colours, received seven wounds
from arrows and lances, in the defence of his master, and on his
part did much injury to the enemy and assassins. When his wounds
were healed, he was sent to King Henry II. by William earl of
Gloucester, in testimony of so great and extraordinary a deed.

A dog, of all animals, is most attached to man, and most easily
distinguishes him; sometimes, when deprived of his master, he
refuses to live, and in his master's defence is bold enough to brave
death; ready, therefore, to die, either with or for his master.

George Crabbe (1754–1832)

Fidelity of the Dog

With eye upraised, his master's looks to scan,
  The joy, the solace and the aid of man;
The rich man's guardian, and the poor man's friend,
  The only creature faithful to the end.

Eleanor Atkinson (1863–1942)

From *Greyfriars Bobby*

Then there was the story of Bobby's devotion to Auld Jack's
memory to be told – the days when he faced starvation rather
than desert that grave, the days when he lay cramped, under the
fallen table-tomb, and his repeated, dramatic escapes from the
Pentland farm. His never-broken silence in the kirkyard was only
to be explained by the unforgotten orders of his dead master. His
intelligent effort to make himself useful to the caretaker had won
indulgence. His ready obedience, good temper, high spirits and
friendliness had made him the special pet of the tenement children
and the Heriot laddies. At the very last Mr. Traill repeated the talk
he had had with the non-commissioned officer from the Castle,
and confessed his own fear of some forlorn end for Bobby. It was
true he was nobody's dog; and he was fascinated by soldiers and
military music, and so perhaps –
  'I'll no' be reconciled to parting – Eh, man, that's what Auld
Jack himself said when he was telling me that the bit dog must be

returned to the sheep-farm: 'It will be sair partin".' Tears stood in the unashamed landlord's eyes.

Glenormiston was pulling Bobby's silkily fringed ears thoughtfully. Through all this talk about his dead master the little dog had not stirred. For the second time that day Bobby's veil was pushed back, first by the most unfortunate laddie in the decaying tenements about Greyfriars, and now by the Lord Provost of the ancient royal burgh and capital of Scotland. And both made the same discovery. Deep-brown pools of love, young Bobby's eyes had dwelt upon Auld Jack. Pools of sad memories they were now, looking out wistfully and patiently upon a masterless world.

'Are you thinking he would be reconciled to be anywhere away from that grave? Look, man!'

'Lord forgive me! I aye thought the wee doggie happy enough.'

After a moment the two men went down from the gallery stairs in silence. Bobby dropped from the bench and fell into a subdued trot at their heels. As they left the cathedral by the door that led into High Street Glenormiston remarked, with a mysterious smile:

'I'm thinking Edinburgh can do better by wee Bobbie than to banish him to the Castle. But wait a bit, man. A kirk is not the place for settling a small dog's affairs.'

The Lord Provost led the way westward along the cathedral's front. On High Street, St. Giles had three doorways. The middle door then gave admittance to the police office; the western opened into the Little Kirk, popularly known as Haddo's Hole. It was into this bare, white-washed chapel that Glenormiston turned to get some restoration drawings he had left on the pulpit. He was explaining them to Mr. Traill when he was interrupted by a murmur and a shuffle, as of many voices and feet, and an odd tap-tap-tapping in the vestibule.

Of all the doorways on the north and south fronts of St. Giles the one to the Little Kirk was nearest the end of George IV Bridge. Confused by the vast size and imposing architecture of the old cathedral, these slum children, in search of the police office, went no farther, but ventured timidly into the open vestibule of Haddo's Hole. Any doubts they might have had about this being the right place were soon dispelled. Bobby heard them and darted out to investigate. And suddenly they were all inside, overwrought Ailie on the floor, clasping the little dog and crying hysterically:

'Bobby's no' deid! Bobby's no' deid! Oh, Maister Traill, ye wullna hae to gie 'im up to the police! Tammy's got the seven shullin's in 'is bonnet!'

And there was small Tammy, crutches dropped and pouring that offering of love and mercy out at the foot of an altar in old St. Giles. Such an astonishing pile of copper coins it was, that it looked to the landlord like the loot of some shopkeeper's change drawer.

'Eh, puir laddie, whaur did ye get it a' noo?' he asked, gravely.

Tammy was very self-possessed and proud. 'The bairnies aroond the kirkyaird gie'd it to pay the police no' to mak' Bobby be deid.'

Mr. Traill flashed a glance at Glenormiston. It was a look at once of triumph and of humility over the Herculean deed of these disinherited children. But the Lord Provost was gazing at that crowd of pale bairns, products of the Old Town's ancient slums, and feeling, in his own person, the civic shame of it ... It was an incredible thing that such a flower of affection should have bloomed so sweetly in such sunless cells. And it was a new gospel at that time, that a dog or a horse or a bird might have its mission in this world of making people kinder and happier.

They were all down on the floor, in the space before the altar, unwashed, uncombed, unconscious of the dirty rags that scarce covered them; quite happy and self-forgetful in the charming friskings and friendly lollings of the well-fed, carefully groomed,

beautiful little dog. Ailie, still so excited that she forgot to be
shy, put Bobby through his pretty tricks. He rolled over and over,
he jumped, he danced to Tammy's whistling of 'Bonnie Dundee',
he walked on his hind legs and louped at a bonnet, he begged, he
lifted his short shagged paw and shook hands. Then he sniffed at
the heap of coins, looked up inquiringly at Mr. Traill, and concluding
that here was some property to be guarded, stood by the 'siller' as
staunchly as a soldier. It was just pure pleasure to watch him.

Very suddenly the Lord Provost changed his mind. A sacred kirk
was the very best place of all to settle this little dog's affairs. The
offering of these children could not be refused. It should lie there,
below the altar, and be consecrated to some other blessed work;
and he would do now and here what he had meant to do elsewhere
and in a quite different way. He lifted Bobby to the pulpit so that
all might see him, and he spoke so that all might understand.

'Are ye kenning' what it is to gie the freedom o' the toon to
grand folk?'

'It's – it's when the bonny Queen comes an' ye gie her the keys
to the burgh gates that are no' here any mair.' Tammy, being in
Heriot's, was a laddie of learning.

'Weel done, laddie. Lang syne there was a wa' aroond Edinburgh
wi' gates in it.' Oh yes, all these bairnies knew that, and the
fragment of it that was still to be seen outside and above the
Grassmarket, with its sentry tower by the old west port. 'Gin a
fey king or ither grand veesitor cam', the Laird Provost an' the
maigestrates gied 'im the keys so he could gang in an' oot at 'is
pleasure. The wa's are a' doon noo, an' the gates no' here ony mair,
but we hae the keys, an' we mak' a show o' gien' 'em to veesitors
wha are vera grand or wise or gude, or juist usefu' by the ordinar'.'

'Maister Gladstone,' said Tammy.

'Ay, we honor the Queen's ministers; an' Miss Nightingale, wha nursed the soldiers i' the war; an' Leddy Burdett-Coutts, wha gies a' her siller an' a' heart to puir folk an' is aye kind to horses and dogs an' singin' birdies; an' we gie the keys to heroes o' the war wha are brave an' faithfu'. An' noo, there's a wee bit beastie. He's weel-behavin', an' isna makin' a blatterin' i' an auld kirkyard. He aye minds what he's bidden to do. He's cheerfu' an' busy, keepin' the proolin' pussies an' vermin frae the sma' birdies i' the nests. He mak's friends o' ilka body, an' he's faithfu'. For a deid man he lo'ed he's gaun hungry; an' he hasna forgotten 'im or left 'im by 'is lane at nicht for mair years than some o' ye are auld. An' gin ye find 'im lyin' canny, an ye tak' a keek into 'is bonny brown eyes, ye can see he's aye greetin'. An' so, ye didna ken why, but ye a' lo'ed the lanely wee – '

'Bobby!' It was an excited breath of a word from the wide-eyed bairns.

'Bobby! Havers! A bittie dog wadna ken what to do wi' keys.'

But Glenormiston was smiling, and these sharp-witted slum bairns exchanged knowing glances. 'Whaur's that sma'– ? He dived into this pocket and that, making a great pretence of searching, until he found a narrow band of new leather, with holes in one end and a stout buckle on the other, and riveted fast in the middle of it was a shining brass plate. Tammy read the inscription aloud:

GREYFRIARS BOBBY
From the Lord Provost
1867 Licensed

John Aubrey (1626–1697)

Faithful in Death

This present Earl of Pembroke (1680) has at Wilton, 52 mastives
and 30 grey-hounds, some beares, and a lyon, and a matter of 60
fellowes more bestiall than they. This Wm. (the founder of this
family) had a little cur-dog which loved him, and the E(arl) loved
the dog. When the Earl dyed the dog would not goe from his
master's dead body, but pined away, and dyed under the hearse; the
picture of which dog is under his picture, in the Gallery at Wilton,
which putts me in mind of a parallel storie in Appain (*Syrian Warr*).

R.C. Lehmann (1856–1929)

To Rufus: A Spaniel

Rufus, a bright New Year! A savoury stew,
Bones, broth and biscuits is prepared for you.
See how it steams in your enamelled dish,
Mixed in each part according to your wish.
Hide in your straw the bones you cannot crunch –
They'll come in handy for tomorrow's lunch;
Abstract with care each tasty scrap of meat,
Remove each biscuit to a fresh retreat
(A dog, I judge, would deem himself disgraced
Who ate a biscuit where he found it placed);
Then muzzle round and make your final sweep,
And sleep, replete, your after-dinner sleep.
High in our hall we've piled the fire with logs
For you, the *doyen* of our corps of dogs.
There, when the stroll that health demands is done,
Your right to ease by due exertion won,
There shall you come, and on your long-haired mat,
Thrice turning round, shall tread the jungle flat,
And rhythmically snoring, dream away
The peaceful evening of your New Year's Day.

Rufus! There are those who hesitate to own
Merits, they say, your master sees alone.
They judge you stupid, for you show no bent
To any poodle-dog accomplishment.
Your stubborn nature never stopped to learn
Tricks by which mumming dogs their biscuits earn.

Men mostly find you, if they change their seat,
Couchant obnoxious to their blundering feet;
Then, when a door is closed, you steadily
Misjudge the side on which you ought to be;
Yelping outside when all your friends are in,
You raise the echoes with your ceaseless din,
Or, always wrong, but turn and turn about,
Howling inside when all the world is out.
They scorn your gestures and interpret ill
Your humble signs of friendship and goodwill.
Laugh at your gambols, and pursue with jeers
The ringlets clustered on your spreading ears;
See without sympathy your sore distress
When Ray obtains the coveted caress,
And you, a jealous lump of growl and glare,
Hide from the world your head beneath a chair.

They say your legs are bandy – so they are:
Nature so formed them that they might go far;
They cannot brook your music; they assail
The joyful quiverings of your stumpy tail –
In short, in one anathema confound
Shape, mind and heart, and all my little hound.
Well, let them rail. If, since your life began,
Beyond the customary lot of man
Staunchness was yours; if of your favourite heart
Malice and scorn could never claim a part;
If in your master, loving while you live,
You own no fault, or own it to forgive;
If, as you lay your head upon his knee,
Your deep-drawn sighs proclaim your sympathy.

If faith and friendship, growing with your age
Speak through your eyes, and all his love engage;
If by that master's wish your life you rule –
If this be folly, Rufus, you're a fool.

Old dog, content you; Rufus, have no fear:
While life is yours and mine your place is here.
And when the day shall come, as come it must,
When Rufus goes to mingle with the dust
(If fate ordains that you shall pass before
To the abhorred and sunless Stygian shore),
I think old Charon, punting through the dark,
Will hear a sudden friendly little bark;
And on the shore he'll mark without a frown
A flap-eared doggie, bandy-legged and brown.
He'll take you in: since watermen are kind,
He'd scorn to leave my little dog behind.

He'll ask no obol, but install you there
On Styx's further bank without a fare.
There shall you sniff his cargoes as they come,
And droop your head, and turn and still be dumb –
Till one fine day, half joyful, half in fear,
You run and prick and recognizing ear,
And last, oh rapture! leaping to his hand,
Salute your master as he steps to land.

Homer, translated by Alexander Pope (1688–1744)

From *The Odyssey*

ARGUS

When wise Ulysses, from his native coasts
Long kept by wars, and long by tempests tossed,
Arrived at last, poor, old, disguised, alone,
To all his friends and even his Queen unknown;
Changed as he was, with age, and toils and cares,
In his own palace forced to ask his bread,
Scorned by those slaves his former bounty fed,
Forgot of all his own domestic crew;
The faithful dog alone his rightful master knew!
Unfed, unhoused, neglected, on the clay
Like an old servant, now cashiered, he lay;
Touched with resentment of ungrateful man,
And longing to behold his ancient lord again.
Him when he saw – he rose, and crawled to meet,
('Twas all he could) and fawned and kissed his feet,
Seized with dumb joy – then
falling by his side,
Owned his returning lord,
looked up and died!

Anon, c. 1393, translated by Eileen Power

From *The Goodman of Paris* (*Le Ménagier de Paris*)

Of domestic animals you shall see how that a greyhound or mastiff or little dog, whether it be on the road, or at a table or in bed, ever keepeth him close to the person from whom he taketh his food and leaveth all the others and is distant and shy with them; and if the dog is afar off, he always has his heart and eye upon his master; even if his master whip him and throw stones at him, the dog followeth, wagging his tail and lying down before his master to appease him, and through rivers, through woods, through thieves and through battles followeth him.

Another ensample may be taken from the dog Macaire, that saw his master slain within a wood, and when he was dead left him not, but lay down in the wood near to the dead man, and by day went to find food afar off and brought it back in his mouth and there returned without eating it, but lay down and drank and ate beside the corpse of his master, all dead within the wood. Afterwards this dog several times fought and attacked the man that had slain his master, and whenever he found him did assail and attack him; and in the end he overbore the man in the fields on the island of Notre-Dame at Paris, and even to this day there be traces there of the lists that were made for the dog and for the field [of battle].

By God, at Niort I saw an old dog, that lay upon the put wherein his master had been buried, that had been slain by the English, and Monseigneur de Berry and a great number of lords were led there to see the marvel of this dog's loyalty and love, that day and night left not the pit, wherein was his master that the English had slain.

And Monseigneur de Berry caused ten francs to be given to
him, the which were delivered to a neighbour to find food for him
all his life.

Robert William Spencer (1769–1834)

Beth Gêlert

The spearmen heard the bugle sound,
  And cheerily smil'd the morn;
And many a brach, and many a hound,
  Obey'd Llewelyn's horn.

And still he blew a louder blast,
  And gave a lustier cheer;
'Come, Gêlert, come, wert never last
  Llewelyn's horn to hear.' –

Oh where does faithful Gêlert roam,
  The flower of all his race;
So true, so brave, a lamb at home,
  A lion in the chase?

'Twas only at Llewelyn's board
  The faithful Gêlert fed;
He watch'd, he served, he cheer'd his lord,
  And sentinel'd his bed.

In sooth he was a peerless hound,
    The gift of royal John;
But now no Gêlert could be found,
    And all the chase rode on.

And now, as o'er the rocks and dells
    The gallant chidings rise,
All Snowdon's craggy chaos yells
    The many-mingled cries!

That day Llewelyn little lov'd
    The chase of hart and hare;
And scant and small the booty prov'd,
    For Gêlert was not there.

Unpleas'd Llewelyn homeward hied;
    When, near the portal seat,
His truant Gêlert he espied
    Bounding his lord to greet.

But when he gain'd his castle door,
    Aghast the chieftain stood;
The hound all o'er was smear'd with gore,
    His lips, his fangs, ran blood.

Llewelyn gaz'd with fierce surprise;
    Unus'd such looks to meet,
The favourite check'd his joyful guise,
    And crouch'd, and licked his feet.

Onward, in haste, Llewelyn pass'd,
    And on went Gêlert too;
And still, where'er his eyes he cast,
    Fresh blood-gouts shocked his view.

O'erturned his infant's bed he found,
    With bloodstain'd covert rent;
And all around the walls and ground
    With recent blood besprent.

He call'd his child, no voice replied –
    He search'd with terror wild;
Blood, blood he found on every side,
    But nowhere found his child.

'Hellhound! my child's by thee devour'd,'
    The frantic father cried,
And to the hilt his vengeful sword
    He plung'd in Gêlert's side.

His suppliant looks, as prone he fell,
    No pity could impart;
But still his Gêlert's dying yell
    Pass'd heavy o'er his heart.

Arous'd by Gêlert's dying yell,
    Some slumberer waken'd nigh; –
What words the parent's joy could tell
    To hear his infant's cry!

Conceal'd beneath a tumbled heap
   His hurried search had miss'd,
All glowing from his rosy sleep,
   The cherub boy he kissed.

Nor scath had he, nor harm, nor dread;
   But, the same couch beneath,
Lay a gaunt wolf, all torn and dead,
   Tremendous still in death.

Ah, what was then Llewelyn's pain!
   For now the truth was clear;
His gallant hound the wolf had slain,
   To save Llewelyn's heir.

Vain, vain was all Llewelyn's woe:
   'Best of thy kind, adieu!
The frantic blow which laid thee low
   This heart shall ever rue.'

And now a gallant tomb they raise,
   With costly sculpture deck'd;
And marbles storied with his praise
   Poor Gêlert's bones protect.

There never could the spearman pass,
   Or forester, unmov'd;
There, oft the tear-besprinkled grass
   Llewelyn's sorrow prov'd.

And there he hung his horn and spear,
  And there, as evening fell,
In fancy's ear, he oft would hear
  Poor Gêlert's dying yell.

And, till great Snowdon's rocks grow old,
  And cease the storm to brave,
The consecrated spot shall hold
  The name of 'Gêlert's grave'.

Mark Twain (1835–1910)

From *A Dog's Tale*

One day I was standing a watch in the nursery. That is to say, I
was asleep on the bed. The baby was asleep in the crib, which was
alongside the bed, on the side next the fireplace. It was the kind of
crib that has a lofty tent over it made of gauzy stuff that you can
see through. The nurse was out, and we two sleepers were alone.
A spark from the wood-fire was shot out, and it lit on the slope of
the tent. I suppose a quiet interval followed, then a scream from
the baby awoke me, and there was that tent flaming up toward the
ceiling! Before I could think, I sprang to the floor in my fright, and
in a second was half-way to the door; but in the next half-second
my mother's farewell was sounding in my ears, and I was back on
the bed again. I reached my head through the flames and dragged
the baby out by the waist-band, and tugged it along, and we fell to
the floor together in a cloud of smoke; I snatched a new hold, and
dragged the screaming little creature along and out at the door and

around the bend of the hall, and was still tugging away, all excited and happy and proud, when the master's voice shouted:

'Begone you cursed beast!' and I jumped to save myself; but he was furiously quick, and chased me up, striking furiously at me with his cane, I dodging this way and that, in terror, and at last a strong blow fell upon my left foreleg, which made me shriek and fall, for the moment, helpless; the cane went up for another blow, but never descended, for the nurse's voice rang wildly out, 'The nursery's on fire!' and the master rushed away in that direction, and my other bones were saved.

The pain was cruel, but no matter, I must not lose any time; he might come back at any moment; so I limped on three legs to the other end of the hall, where there was a dark little stairway leading up into a garret where old boxes and such things were kept, as I had heard say, and where people seldom went. I managed to climb up there, then I searched my way through the dark among the piles of things, and hid in the secretest place I could find. It was foolish to be afraid there, yet still I was; so afraid that I held in and hardly even whimpered, though it would have been such a comfort to whimper, because that eases the pain, you know. But I could lick my leg, and that did some good.

For half an hour there was a commotion downstairs, and shoutings, and rushing footsteps, and then there was quiet again. Quiet for some minutes, and that was grateful to my spirit, for then my fears began to go down; and fears are worse than pains – oh, much worse. Then came a sound that froze me. They were calling me – calling me by name – hunting for me!

It was muffled by distance, but that could not take the terror out of it, and it was the most dreadful sound to me that I had ever heard. It went all about, everywhere, down there: along the halls, through all the rooms, in both stories and in the basement and the cellar; then outside, and farther and farther away – then back, and all about the house again, and I thought it would never, never stop. But at last it did, hours and hours after the vague twilight of the garret had long ago been blotted out by black darkness.

Then in that blessed stillness my terrors fell little by little away, and I was at peace and slept. It was a good rest I had, but I woke before the twilight had come again. I was feeling fairly comfortable, and I could think out a plan now. I made a very good one; which was, to creep down, all the way down the back stairs, and hide behind the cellar door, and slip out and escape when the iceman came at dawn, while he was inside filling the refrigerator; then I would hide all day, and start on my journey when night came; my journey to – well, anywhere where they would not know me and betray me to the master. I was feeling almost cheerful now; then suddenly I thought: Why, what would life be without my puppy!

That was despair. There was no plan for me; I saw that; I must stay where I was; stay, and wait, and take what might come – it was not my affair; that was what life is – my mother had said it. Then – well, then the calling began again! All my sorrows came back. I said to myself, the master will never forgive. I did not know what I had done to make him so bitter and so unforgiving, yet I judged it was something a dog could not understand, but which was clear to a man and dreadful.

They called and called – days and nights, it seemed to me. So long that the hunger and thirst near drove me mad, and I recognized that I was getting very weak. When you are this way you sleep a great deal, and I did. Once I woke in an awful fright – it seemed to me that the calling was right there in the garret! And so it was: it was Sadie's voice, and she was crying; my name was falling from her lips all broken, poor thing, and I could not believe my ears for the joy of it when I heard her say:

'Come back to us – oh, come back to us, and forgive – it is all so sad without our – "

I broke in with SUCH a grateful little yelp, and the next moment Sadie was plunging and stumbling through the darkness and the lumber and shouting for the family to hear, 'She's found, she's found!'

Walter Savage Landor (1775–1864)

Answer to a Dog's Invitation

Faithfullest of a faithful race,
Plainly I read it in thy face
Thous wishest me to mount the stairs
And leave behind me all my cares.
No; I shall never see again
Her who now sails across the main:
Nor wilt thou ever, as before
Rear two white feet against her door.
Therefore do thou nor whine nor roam,
But rest thee and curl round at home.

James Douglas

If the history of all the dogs who have loved and been loved by the race of man could be written, each history of a dog would resemble all the other histories. It would be a love story.

Rudyard Kipling (1865–1936)

Garm: A Hostage

One night, a very long time ago, I drove to an Indian military
cantonment called Mian Mir to see amateur theatricals. At the back
of the Infantry barracks a soldier, his cap over one eye, rushed in
front of the horses and shouted that he was a dangerous highway
robber. As a matter of fact, he was a friend of mine, so I told him
to go home before any one caught him; but he fell under the pole,
and I heard voices of a military guard in search of some one.

The driver and I coaxed him into the carriage, drove home
swiftly, undressed him and put him to bed, where he waked next
morning with a sore headache, very much ashamed. When his
uniform was cleaned and dried, and he had been shaved and
washed and made neat, I drove him back to barracks with his arm
in a fine white sling, and reported that I had accidentally run over
him. I did not tell this story to my friend's sergeant, who was a
hostile and unbelieving person, but to his lieutenant, who did not
know us quite so well.

Three days later my friend came to call, and at his heels
slobbered and fawned one of the finest bull-terriers – of the old-
fashioned breed, two parts bull and one terrier – that I had ever
set eyes on. He was pure white, with a fawn-coloured saddle just
behind his neck, and a fawn diamond at the root of his thin whippy
tail. I had admired him distantly for more than a year; and Vixen,
my own fox-terrier, knew him too, but did not approve.

'E's for you,' said my friend; but he did not look as though he
liked parting with him.

'Nonsense! That dog's worth more than most men, Stanley,'
I said.

"E's that and more. 'Tention!'

The dog rose on his hind legs, and stood upright for a full minute. 'Eyes right!'

He sat on his haunches and turned his head sharp to the right. At a sign he rose and barked thrice. Then he shook hands with his right paw and bounded lightly to my shoulder. Here he made himself into a necktie, limp and lifeless, hanging down on either side of my neck. I was told to pick him up and throw him in the air. He fell with a howl, and held up one leg

'Part o' the trick,' said his owner. 'You're going to die now. Dig yourself your little grave an' shut your little eye.'

Still limping, the dog hobbled to the garden-edge, dug a hole and lay down in it. When told that he was cured, he jumped out, wagging his tail, and whining for applause. He was put through half-a-dozen other tricks, such as showing how he would hold a man safe (I was that man, and he sat down before me, his teeth bared, ready to spring), and how he would stop eating at the word of command. I had no more than finished praising him when my friend made a gesture that stopped the dog as though he had been shot, took a piece of blue-ruled canteen-paper from his helmet, handed it to me and ran away, while the dog looked after him and howled. I read:

Sir – I give you the dog because of what you got me out of. He is the best I know, for I made him myself, and he is as good as a man. Please do not give him too much to eat, and please do not give him back to me, for I'm not going to take him, if you will keep him. So please do not try to give him back any more. I have kept his name back, so you can call him anything and he will answer. But please do not give him back. He can kill a man as easy as anything, but please do not give him too much meat. He knows more than a man.

Vixen sympathetically joined her shrill little yap to the bull-terrier's despairing cry, and I was annoyed, for I knew that a man who cares for dogs is one thing, but a man who loves one dog is quite another. Dogs are at the best no more than verminous vagrants, self-scratchers, foul feeders and unclean by the law of Moses and Mohammed; but a dog with whom one lives alone for at least six months in the year; a free thing, tied to you so strictly by love that without you he will not stir or exercise; a patient, temperate, humorous, wise soul, who knows your moods before you know them yourself, is not a dog under any ruling.

I had Vixen, who was all my dog to me; and I felt what my friend must have felt, at tearing out his heart in this style and leaving it in my garden. However, the dog understood clearly enough that I was his master, and did not follow the soldier. As soon as he drew breath I made much of him, and Vixen, yelling with jealousy, flew at him. Had she been of his own sex, he might have cheered himself with a fight, but he only looked worriedly when she nipped his deep iron sides, laid his heavy head on my knee and howled anew. I meant to dine at the Club that night; but as darkness drew in, and the dog snuffed through the empty house like a child trying to recover from a fit of sobbing, I felt that I could not leave him to suffer his first evening alone. So we fed at home, Vixen on one side, and the stranger-dog on the other; she watching his every mouthful, and saying explicitly what she thought of his table manners, which were much better than hers.

It was Vixen's custom, till the weather grew hot, to sleep in my bed, her head on the pillow like a Christian; and when morning came I would always find that the little thing had braced her feet against the wall and pushed me to the very edge of the cot. This night she hurried to bed purposefully, every hair up, one eye on the stranger, who had dropped on a mat in a helpless, hopeless sort of way, all four feet spread out, sighing heavily. She settled her head on the pillow several times, to show her little airs and graces, and struck up her usual whiney sing-song before slumber. The stranger-dog softly edged toward me. I put out my hand and he licked it. Instantly my wrist was between Vixen's teeth, and her warning aaarh! said as plainly as speech, that if I took any further notice of the stranger she would bite.

I caught her behind her fat neck with my left hand, shook her severely and said:

'Vixen, if you do that again you'll be put into the verandah. Now, remember!'

She understood perfectly, but the minute I released her she mouthed my right wrist once more, and waited with her ears back and all her body flattened, ready to bite. The big dog's tail thumped the floor in a humble and peace-making way.

I grabbed Vixen a second time, lifted her out of bed like a rabbit (she hated that and yelled) and, as I had promised, set her out in the verandah with the bats and the moonlight. At this she howled. Then she used coarse language – not to me, but to the bull-terrier – till she coughed with exhaustion. Then she ran round the house trying every door. Then she went off to the stables and barked as though some one were stealing the horses, which was an old trick of hers. Last she returned, and her snuffing yelp said, 'I'll be good! Let me in and I'll be good!'

She was admitted and flew to her pillow. When she was quieted I whispered to the other dog, 'You can lie on the foot of the bed'. The bull jumped up at once, and though I felt Vixen quiver with rage, she knew better than to protest. So we slept till the morning, and they had early breakfast with me, bite for bite, till the horse came round and we went for a ride. I don't think the bull had ever followed a horse before. He was wild with excitement, and Vixen,

as usual, squealed and scuttered and scooted, and took charge of
the procession.

There was one corner of a village near by, which we generally
passed with caution, because all the yellow pariah-dogs of the place
gathered about it.

They were half-wild, starving beasts, and though utter cowards,
yet where nine or ten of them get together they will mob and kill
and eat an English dog. I kept a whip with a long lash for them.

That morning they attacked Vixen, who, perhaps of design, had
moved from beyond my horse's shadow.

The bull was ploughing along in the dust, fifty yards behind,
rolling in his run, and smiling as bull-terriers will. I heard Vixen
squeal; half a dozen of the curs closed in on her; a white streak
came up behind me; a cloud of dust rose near Vixen and, when it
cleared, I saw one tall pariah with his back broken, and the bull
wrenching another to earth. Vixen retreated to the protection
of my whip, and the bull paddled back smiling more than ever,
covered with the blood of his enemies. That decided me to call him
'Garm of the Bloody Breast', who was a great person in his time, or
'Garm' for short; so, leaning forward, I told him what his temporary
name would be. He looked up while I repeated it, and then raced
away. I shouted 'Garm!' He stopped, raced back and came up to ask
my will.

Then I saw that my soldier friend was right, and that that dog
knew and was worth more than a man. At the end of the ride I gave
an order which Vixen knew and hated: 'Go away and get washed!'
I said. Garm understood some part of it, and Vixen interpreted the
rest, and the two trotted off together soberly. When I went to the
back verandah Vixen had been washed snowy-white, and was very
proud of herself, but the dog-boy would not touch Garm on any
account unless I stood by. So I waited while he was being scrubbed,

and Garm, with the soap creaming on the top of his broad head, looked at me to make sure that this was what I expected him to endure. He knew perfectly that the dog-boy was only obeying orders.

'Another time,' I said to the dog-boy, 'you will wash the great dog with Vixen when I send them home.'

'Does he know?' said the dog-boy, who understood the ways of dogs.

'Garm,' I said, 'another time you will be washed with Vixen.'

I knew that Garm understood. Indeed, next washing-day, when Vixen as usual fled under my bed, Garm stared at the doubtful dog-boy in the verandah, stalked to the place where he had been washed last time and stood rigid in the tub.

But the long days in my office tried him sorely. We three would drive off in the morning at half-past eight and come home at six or later. Vixen, knowing the routine of it, went to sleep under my table; but the confinement ate into Garm's soul. He generally sat on the verandah looking out on the Mall; and well I knew what he expected.

Sometimes a company of soldiers would move along on their way to the Fort, and Garm rolled forth to inspect them; or an officer in uniform entered into the office, and it was pitiful to see poor Garm's welcome to the cloth – not the man. He would leap at him, and sniff and bark joyously, then run to the door and back again. One afternoon I heard him bay with a full throat – a thing I had never heard before – and he disappeared. When I drove into my garden at the end of the day a soldier in white uniform scrambled over the wall at the far end, and the Garm that met me was a joyous dog. This happened twice or thrice a week for a month.

I pretended not to notice, but Garm knew and Vixen knew. He would glide homewards from the office about four o'clock, as though he were only going to look at the scenery, and this he did so quietly that but for Vixen I should not have noticed him. The jealous little dog under the table would give a sniff and a snort, just loud enough to call my attention to the flight. Garm might go out forty times in the day and Vixen would never stir, but when he slunk off to see his true master in my garden she told me in her own tongue. That was the one sign she made to prove that Garm did not altogether belong to the family. They were the best of friends at all times, but, Vixen explained that I was never to forget Garm did not love me as she loved me.

I never expected it. The dog was not my dog, could never be my dog – and I knew he was as miserable as his master who tramped eight miles a day to see him. So it seemed to me that the sooner the two were reunited the better for all. One afternoon I sent Vixen home alone in the dog-cart (Garm had gone before), and rode over to cantonments to find another friend of mine, who was an Irish soldier and a great friend of the dog's master.

I explained the whole case, and wound up with:

'And now Stanley's in my garden crying over his dog. Why doesn't he take him back? They're both unhappy.'

'Unhappy! There's no sense in the little man any more. But 'tis his fit.'

'What is his fit? He travels fifty miles a week to see the brute, and he pretends not to notice me when he sees me on the road; and I'm as unhappy as he is. Make him take the dog back.'

'It's his penance he's set himself. I told him by way of a joke, after you'd run over him so convenient that night, whin he was drunk – I said if he was a Catholic he'd do penance. Off he went wid that fit in his little head an' a dose of fever, an nothin'would suit but givin' you the dog as a hostage.'

'Hostage for what? I don't want hostages from Stanley.'

'For his good behaviour. He's keepin' straight now, the way it's no pleasure to associate wid him.'

'Has he taken the pledge?'

'If 'twas only that I need not care. Ye can take the pledge for three months on an' off. He sez he'll never see the dog again, an' so mark you, he'll keep straight for evermore. Ye know his fits? Well, this is wan of them. How's the dog takin' it?'

'Like a man. He's the best dog in India. Can't you make Stanley take him back?'

'I can do no more than I have done. But ye know his fits. He's just doin' his penance. What will he do when he goes to the Hills? The doctor's put him on the list.'

It is the custom in India to send a certain number of invalids from each regiment up to stations in the Himalayas for the hot weather; and though the men ought to enjoy the cool and the comfort, they miss the society of the barracks down below, and do their best to come back or to avoid going. I felt that this move would bring matters to a head, so I left Terrence hopefully, though he called after me 'He won't take the dog, sorry. You can lay your month's pay on that. Ye know his fits.'

I never pretended to understand Private Ortheris; and so I did the next best thing – I left him alone.

That summer the invalids of the regiment to which my friend belonged were ordered off to the Hills early, because the doctors thought marching in the cool of the day would do them good. Their route lay south to a place called Umballa, a hundred and twenty miles or more. Then they would turn east and march up into the hills to Kasauli or Dugshai or Subathoo. I dined with the officers the night before they left – they were marching at five in the morning. It was midnight when I drove into my garden, and surprised a white figure flying over the wall.

'That man,' said my butler, 'has been here since nine, making talk to that dog. He is quite mad.'

'I did not tell him to go away because he has been here many times before, and because the dog-boy told me that if I told him to go away, that great dog would immediately slay me. He did not wish to speak to the Protector of the Poor, and he did not ask for anything to eat or drink.'

'Kadir Buksh,' said I, 'that was well done, for the dog would surely have killed thee. But I do not think the white soldier will come any more.'

Garm slept ill that night and whimpered in his dreams. Once he sprang up with a clear, ringing bark, and I heard him wag his tail till it waked him and the bark died out in a howl. He had dreamed he was with his master again, and I nearly cried. It was all Stanley's silly fault.

The first halt which the detachment of invalids made was some miles from their barracks, on the Amritsar road, and ten miles distant from my house. By a mere chance one of the officers drove back for another good dinner at the Club (cooking on the line of march is always bad), and there I met him. He was a particular friend of mine, and I knew that he knew how to love a dog properly. His pet was a big fat retriever who was going up to the Hills for his health, and, though it was still April, the round, brown brute puffed and panted in the Club verandah as though he would burst.

'It's amazing,' said the officer, 'what excuses these invalids of mine make to get back to barracks. There's a man in my company now asked me for leave to go back to cantonments to pay a debt he'd forgotten. I was so taken by the idea I let him go, and he jingled off in an ekka as pleased as Punch. Ten miles to pay a debt! Wonder what it was really?'

'If you'll drive me home I think I can show you,' I said.

So he went over to my house in his dog-cart with the retriever; and on the way I told him the story of Garm.

'I was wondering where that brute had gone to. He's the best dog in the regiment,' said my friend. 'I offered the little fellow twenty rupees for him a month ago. But he's a hostage, you say, for Stanley's good conduct. Stanley's one of the best men I have when he chooses.'

'That's the reason why,' I said. 'A second-rate man wouldn't have taken things to heart as he has done.'

We drove in quietly at the far end of the garden, and crept round the house. There was a place close to the wall all grown about with tamarisk trees, where I knew Garm kept his bones. Even Vixen was not allowed to sit near it. In the full Indian moonlight I could see a white uniform bending over the dog.

'Good-bye, old man,' we could not help hearing Stanley's voice.'For 'Eving's sake don't get bit and go mad by any measly pi-dog. But you can look after yourself, old man. You don't get drunk an'run about 'ittin' your friends. You takes your bones an' you eats your biscuit, an' you kills your enemy like a gentleman. I'm goin' away – don't 'owl – I'm goin' off to Kasauli, where I won't see you no more.'

I could hear him holding Garm's nose as the dog threw it up to the stars.

'You'll stay here an' be'ave, an' – an' I'll go away an' try to be'ave, an' I don't know 'ow to leave you. I don't know – '

'I think this is damn silly,' said the officer, patting his foolish fubsy old retriever. He called to the private, who leaped to his feet, marched forward and saluted.

'You here?' said the officer, turning away his head.

'Yes, sir, but I'm just goin' back.'

'I shall be leaving here at eleven in my cart. You come with me. I can't have sick men running about fall over the place. Report yourself at eleven, here.'

We did not say much when we went indoors, but the officer muttered and pulled his retriever's ears.

He was a disgraceful, overfed doormat of a dog; and when he waddled off to my cookhouse to be fed, I had a brilliant idea.

At eleven o'clock that officer's dog was nowhere to be found, and you never heard such a fuss as his owner made. He called and shouted and grew angry, and hunted through my garden for half an hour.

Then I said:

'He's sure to turn up in the morning. Send a man in by rail, and I'll find the beast and return him.'

'Beast?' said the officer. 'I value that dog considerably more than I value any man I know. It's all very fine for you to talk – your dog's here.'

So she was – under my feet – and, had she been missing, food and wages would have stopped in my house till her return. But some people grow fond of dogs not worth a cut of the whip. My friend had to drive away at last with Stanley in the back seat; and then the dog-boy said to me:

'What kind of animal is Bullen Sahib's dog? Look at him!'

I went to the boy's hut, and the fat old reprobate was lying on a mat carefully chained up. He must have heard his master calling for twenty minutes, but had not even attempted to join him.

'He has no face,' said the dog-boy scornfully. 'He is a punniar-kooter (a spaniel). He never tried to get that cloth off his jaws when his master called. Now Vixen-baba would have jumped through the window, and that Great Dog would have slain me with his muzzled mouth. It is true that there are many kinds of dogs.'

Next evening who should turn up but Stanley. The officer had sent him back fourteen miles by rail with a note begging me to return the retriever if I had found him, and, if I had not, to offer huge rewards. The last train to camp left at half-past ten, and Stanley, stayed till ten talking to Garm. I argued and entreated, and even threatened to shoot the bull-terrier, but the little man was as firm as a rock, though I gave him a good dinner and talked to him most severely. Garm knew as well as I that this was the last time he could hope to see his man, and followed Stanley like a shadow. The retriever said nothing, but licked his lips after his meal and waddled off without so much as saying 'Thank you' to the disgusted dog-boy.

So that last meeting was over, and I felt as wretched as Garm, who moaned in his sleep all night. When we went to the office he found a place under the table close to Vixen, and dropped flat till it was time to go home. There was no more running out into the verandahs, no slinking away for stolen talks with Stanley. As the weather grew warmer the dogs were forbidden to run beside the cart, but sat at my side on the seat, Vixen with her head under the crook of my left elbow, and Garm hugging the left handrail.

Here Vixen was ever in great form. She had to attend to all the moving traffic, such as bullock-carts that blocked the way, and camels and led ponies; as well as to keep up her dignity when she passed low friends running in the dust. She never yapped for yapping's sake, but her shrill, high bark was known all along the Mall, and other men's terriers ki-yied in reply, and bullock-drivers looked over their shoulders and gave us the road with a grin.

But Garm cared for none of these things. His big eyes were on the horizon and his terrible mouth was shut. There was another dog in the office who belonged to my chief. We called him 'Bob the Librarian,' because he always imagined vain rats behind the bookshelves, and in hunting for them would drag out half the old newspaper-files. Bob was a well-meaning idiot, but Garm did not encourage him. He would slide his head round the door panting,'Rats! Come along Garm!' and Garm would shift one forepaw over the other, and curl himself round, leaving Bob to whine at a most uninterested back. The office was nearly as cheerful as a tomb in those days.

Once, and only once, did I see Garm at all contented with his surroundings. He had gone for an unauthorised walk with Vixen early one Sunday morning, and a very young and foolish artilleryman (his battery had just moved to that part of the world) tried to steal them both. Vixen, of course, knew better than to take food from soldiers, and, besides, she had just finished her breakfast. So she trotted back with a large piece of the mutton that they issue to our troops, laid it down on my verandah, and looked up to see what I thought. I asked her where Garm was, and she ran in front of the horse to show me the way.

About a mile up the road we came across our artilleryman sitting very stiffly on the edge of a culvert with a greasy handkerchief on his knees. Garm was in front of him, looking rather pleased. When the man moved leg or hand, Garm bared his teeth in silence. A broken string hung from his collar, and the other half of it lay, all warm, in the artilleryman's still hand. He explained to me, keeping his eyes straight in front of him, that he had met this dog (he called him awful names) walking alone, and was going to take him to the Fort to be killed for a masterless pariah.

I said that Garm did not seem to me much of a pariah, but that he had better take him to the Fort if he thought best. He said he did not care to do so. I told him to go to the Fort alone. He said he did not want to go at that hour, but would follow my advice as soon as I had called off the dog. I instructed Garm to take him to the Fort, and Garm marched him solemnly up to the gate, one mile and a half under a hot sun, and I told the quarter-guard what had happened; but the young artilleryman was more angry than was at all necessary when they began to laugh. Several regiments, he was told, had tried to steal Garm in their time.

That month the hot weather shut down in earnest, and the dogs slept in the bathroom on the cool wet bricks where the bath is placed. Every morning, as soon as the man filled my bath the two jumped in, and every morning the man filled the bath a second time. I said to him that he might as well fill a small tub specially for the dogs. 'Nay,' said he smiling, 'it is not their custom. They would not understand. Besides, the big bath gives them more space.'

The punkah-coolies who pull the punkahs day and night came to know Garm intimately. He noticed that when the swaying fan stopped I would call out to the coolie and bid him pull with a long stroke. If the man still slept I would wake him up. He discovered, too, that it was a good thing to lie in the wave of air under the punkah. Maybe Stanley had taught him all about this in barracks. At any rate, when the punkah stopped, Garm would first growl and cock his eye at the rope, and if that did not wake the man it nearly always did – he would tiptoe forth and talk in the sleeper's ear. Vixen was a clever little dog, but she could never connect the punkah and the coolie; so Garm gave me grateful hours of cool sleep. But – he was utterly wretched – as miserable as a human being; and in his misery he clung so closely to me that other men noticed it, and were envious. If I moved from one room to another Garm followed; if my pen stopped scratching, Garm's head was thrust into my hand; if I turned, half awake, on the pillow, Garm was up and at my side, for he knew that I was his only link with his master, and day and night, and night and day, his eyes asked one question – 'When is this going to end?'

Living with the dog as I did, I never noticed that he was more than ordinarily upset by the hot weather, till one day at the Club a man said: 'That dog of yours will die in a week or two. He's a shadow.' Then I dosed Garm with iron and quinine, which he hated; and I felt very anxious. He lost his appetite, and Vixen was allowed to eat his dinner under his eyes. Even that did not make him swallow, and we held a consultation on him, of the best man-doctor in the place; a lady-doctor, who cured the sick wives of kings; and the Deputy Inspector-General of the veterinary service of all India. They pronounced upon his symptoms, and I told them his story, and Garm lay on a sofa licking my hand.

'He's dying of a broken heart,' said the lady-doctor suddenly.

"Pon my word,' said the Deputy Inspector General, 'I believe Mrs. Macrae is perfectly right as usual.'

The best man-doctor in the place wrote a prescription, and the veterinary Deputy Inspector-General went over it afterwards to be sure that the drugs were in the proper dog-proportions; and that was the first time in his life that our doctor ever allowed his prescriptions to be edited. It was a strong tonic, and it put the dear boy on his feet for a week or two; then he lost flesh again. I asked a man I knew to take him up to the Hills with him when he went, and the man came to the door with his kit packed on the top of the carriage. Garm took in the situation at one red glance. The hair rose along his back; he sat down in front of me and delivered the most awful growl I have ever heard in the jaws of a dog. I shouted to my friend to get away at once, and as soon as the carriage was out of the garden Garm laid his head on my knee and whined. So I knew his answer, and devoted myself to getting Stanley's address in the Hills.

My turn to go to the cool came late in August. We were allowed thirty days' holiday in a year, if no one fell sick, and we took it as we could be spared. My chief and Bob the Librarian had their holiday first, and when they were gone I made a calendar, as I always did, and hung it up at the head of my cot, tearing off one day at a time till they returned. Vixen had gone up to the Hills with me five times before; and she appreciated the cold and the damp and the beautiful wood fires there as much as I did.

'Garm,' I said, 'we are going back to Stanley at Kasauli. Kasauli – Stanley; Stanley Kasauli.' And I repeated it twenty times. It was not Kasauli really, but another place. Still I remembered what Stanley had said in my garden on the last night, and I dared not change the name. Then Garm began to tremble; then he barked; and then he leaped up at me, frisking and wagging his tail.

'Not now,' I said, holding up my hand. 'When I say 'Go,' we'll go, Garm.' I pulled out the little blanket coat and spiked collar that Vixen always wore up in the Hills to protect her against sudden chills and thieving leopards, and I let the two smell them and talk it over. What they said of course I do not know; but it made a new dog of Garm. His eyes were bright; and he barked joyfully when I spoke to him. He ate his food, and he killed his rats for the next three weeks, and when he began to whine I had only to say 'Stanley – Kasauli; Kasauli – Stanley,' to wake him up. I wish I had thought of it before.

My chief came back, all brown with living in the open air, and very angry at finding it so hot in the plains. That same afternoon we three and Kadir Buksh began to pack for our month's holiday, Vixen rolling in and out of the bullock-trunk twenty times a minute, and Garm grinning all over and thumping on the floor with his tail. Vixen knew the routine of travelling as well as she knew my office-work. She went to the station, singing songs, on the front seat of the carriage, while Garm sat with me. She hurried into the railway carriage, saw Kadir Buksh make up my bed for the night, got her drink of water, and curled up with her black-patch eye on the tumult of the platform. Garm followed her (the crowd gave him a lane all to himself) and sat down on the pillows with his eyes blazing, and his tail a haze behind him.

We came to Umballa in the hot misty dawn, four or five men, who had been working hard for eleven months, shouting for our dales – the two-horse travelling carriages that were to take us up to Kalka at the foot of the Hills. It was all new to Garm. He did not understand carriages where you lay at full length on your bedding, but Vixen knew and hopped into her place at once; Garm following. The Kalka Road, before the railway was built, was about forty-seven miles long, and the horses were changed every eight miles. Most of them jibbed, and kicked and plunged, but they had to go, and they went rather better than usual for Garm's deep bay in their rear.

There was a river to be forded, and four bullocks pulled the carriage, and Vixen stuck her head out of the sliding-door and nearly fell into the water while she gave directions. Garm was silent and curious, and rather needed reassuring about Stanley and Kasauli. So we rolled, barking and yelping, into Kalka for lunch, and Garm ate enough for two.

After Kalka the road wound among the hills, and we took a curricle with half-broken ponies, which were changed every six miles. No one dreamed of a railroad to Simla in those days, for it was seven thousand feet up in the air. The road was more than fifty miles long, and the regulation pace was just as fast as the ponies could go. Here, again, Vixen led Garm from one carriage to the other; jumped into the back seat, and shouted. A cool breath from the snows met us about five miles out of Kalka, and she whined for her coat, wisely fearing a chill on the liver. I had had one made for Garm too, and, as we climbed to the fresh breezes, I put it on, and Garm chewed it uncomprehendingly, but I think he was grateful.

'Hi-yi-yi-yi!' sang Vixen as we shot round the curves; 'Toot-toot-toot!' went the driver's bugle at the dangerous places, and 'yow! yow!' bayed Garm. Kadir Buksh sat on the front seat and smiled. Even he was glad to get away from the heat of the Plains that stewed in the haze behind us. Now and then we would meet a man we knew going down to his work again, and he would say: 'What's it like below?' and I would shout: 'Hotter than cinders. What's it like up above?' and he would shout back: 'Just perfect!' and away we would go.

Suddenly Kadir Buksh said, over his shoulder: 'Here is Solon'; and Garm snored where he lay with his head on my knee. Solon is an unpleasant little cantonment, but it has the advantage of being cool and healthy. It is all bare and windy, and one generally stops at a rest-house nearby for something to eat. I got out and took both dogs with me, while Kadir Buksh made tea. A soldier told, us we should find Stanley 'out there', nodding his head towards a bare, bleak hill.

When we climbed to the top we spied that very Stanley, who had given me all this trouble, sitting on a rock with his face in his hands, and his overcoat hanging loose about him. I never saw anything so lonely and dejected in my life as this one little man, crumpled up and thinking, on the great gray hillside.

Here Garm left me.

He departed without a word, and, so far as I could see, without moving his legs. He flew through the air bodily, and I heard the whack of him as he flung himself at Stanley, knocking the little man clean over. They rolled on the ground together, shouting, and yelping, and hugging. I could not see which was dog and which was man, till Stanley got up and whimpered.

He told me that he had been suffering from fever at intervals, and was very weak. He looked all he said, but even while I watched, both man and dog plumped out to their natural sizes, precisely as dried apples swell in water. Garm was on his shoulder, and his breast and feet all at the same time, so that Stanley spoke all through a cloud of Garm – gulping, sobbing, slavering Garm. He did not say anything that I could understand, except that he had fancied he was going to die, but that now he was quite well, and that he was not going to give up Garm any more to anybody under the rank of Beelzebub.

Then he said he felt hungry, and thirsty and happy.

We went down to tea at the rest-house, where Stanley stuffed himself with sardines and raspberry jam, and beer, and cold mutton and pickles, when Garm wasn't climbing over him; and then Vixen and I went on.

Garm saw how it was at once. He said good-bye to me three times, giving me both paws one after another, and leaping on to my shoulder. He further escorted us, singing Hosannas at the top of his voice, a mile down the road. Then he raced back to his own master.

Vixen never opened her mouth, but when the cold twilight came, and we could see the lights of Simla across the hills, she snuffled with her nose at the breast of my ulster. I unbuttoned it, and tucked her inside. Then she gave a contented little sniff, and fell fast asleep, her head on my breast, till we bundled out at Simla, two of the four happiest people in all the world that night.

John Gay (1685–1732)

My Dog

My dog (the trustiest of his kind)
With gratitude inflames my mind:
I mark his true, his faith way,
And in my service copy Tray.

War Dogs

————

Geoffrey Dearmer (1893–1996)

The Turkish Trench Dog

Night held me as I crawled and scrambled near
The Turkish lines. Above, the mocking stars
Silvered the curving parapet, and clear
Cloud-latticed beams o'erflecked the land with bars;
I, crouching, lay between
Tense-listening armies, peering through the night,
Twin giants bound by tentacles unseen.
Here in dim-shadowed light
I saw him, as a sudden movement turned
His eyes towards me, glowing eyes that burned
A moment ere his snuffling muzzle found
My trail; and then as serpents mesmerise
He chained me with those unrelenting eyes,
That muscle-sliding rhythm, knit and bound
In spare-limbed symmetry, those perfect jaws
And soft-approaching pitter-patter paws.
Nearer and nearer like a wolf he crept –
That moment had my swift revolver leapt –
But terror seized me, terror born of shame
Brought flooding revelation. For he came
As one who offers comradeship deserved,
An open ally of the human race,
And sniffing at my prostrate form unnerved
He licked my face!

Dorothea St Hill Bourne

From 'They Also Serve'

Somewhere in Scotland overlooking the sea is a grave which
bears the inscription: '24th July 1944. Bamse, Faithful Friend of
all on board Thorod. Largest Dog of all the Allied Forces.' On
the grave some British children placed a Union Jack, but the flag
which should have been there was the Norwegian, for Bamse was
Norwegian born and served in a Norwegian ship.

Before the war, Bamse, a huge St Bernard, lived happily in
Norway with his master, Commander Erling Hafto, of the
Royal Norwegian Navy. He was the devoted playmate of the
Commander's children. His special charge was Vigdis, the youngest
of them all, and from the time she was three Bamse acted almost as
a nurse. Once when Vigdis was ill Bamse guarded the sick-room,
hardly leaving the child's side for twelve days.

When the war came and Commander Hafto joined his ship,
Bamse went with him. He at once decided he was in charge of his
shipmates just as he had been of his small mistress.

The big dog was always worried when any of the crew was
ashore, and would often set out on his own to round them up to
make sure they were back in good time. He knew all their favourite
haunts, and would visit each one in turn, seeking out his shipmates.
He would even queue up and board the right bus to take him to
more distant cafes!

Bamse was once confined to barracks for fighting another dog.
As soon as he was released, Bamse went ashore, sought out his late
opponent, picked him up by the scruff of his neck and dropped
him over the side of the quay. Bamse then returned to his ship.

Gerald of Wales (twelfth century)

From *The Journey through Wales*

In this wood of Coleshulle, a young Welshman was killed while passing through the king's army; the greyhound who accompanied him did not desert his master's corpse for eight days, though without food; but faithfully defended it from the attacks of dogs, wolves and birds of prey, with a wonderful attachment. What son to his father, what Nisus to Euryalus, what Polynices to Tydeus, what Orestes to Pylades, would have shewn such an affectionate regard? As a mark of favour to the dog, who was almost starved to death, the English, although bitter enemies to the Welsh, ordered the body, now nearly putrid, to be deposited in the ground with the accustomed offices of humanity.

Joseph Taylor

From *Canine Gratitude*

At the celebrated battle of Bunker's hill, near Boston, in America, the dog of a foot soldier followed his master unperceived into the midst of the battle, and remained there some time during the heat of the engagement. When the wounded were carried off the field, the soldier who belonged to the dog unhappily lost his leg in the action, and was one of the first ordered to be taken care of; when, as if by mutual sympathy, his poor dog was seen limping after him, having likewise had one of his legs shot off. The gallant soldier, notwithstanding his sufferings, was not unmindful of his poor dog, whom, when he beheld bleeding in a most dreadful manner, humbly requested the poor animal might be taken care of, and permitted to go with him to the hospital. This request was very humanely complied with by the surgeon, who ordered one of his assistants to dress the poor beast's stump. In a short time both man and dog so far recovered, as to be able to hobble about, with the loss of their legs. The soldier was soon after sent a pensioner to Chelsea College; and the grateful dog still accompanied his master to the desired haven, where, in commemoration of the battle, he was christened Bunker. For several years after he used to hop about the walks of the hospital, sleep on the benches and play with the pensioners. The neighbouring gentry would frequently take a walk on purpose, as they used to express it – 'to see the poor dog who lost his leg in the battle of Bunker's hill'.

E.F. Coote Lake

A Little Flanders Tyke

Just a little slip o' khaki, as I took a fancy to,
With a kindly, rather wistful eye – a gentleman all through,
Like another slip in khaki, with a brass band round 'is cap,
'Oo would walk about among us like an ordinary chap.

So I named the mongrel Davy, after Edward Prince of Wales,
Tho' 'e weren't the exhibition sort of dog you see at sales.
But I took a fancy to 'im when 'e come a-creepin' in,
So I shares out with my Bully, an' I lets 'im lick the tin.

'Is coat – it weren't exactly 'air, it weren't exactly fur;
There are lots o' beggars like 'im – just a yellow Flanders cur.
An' 'is 'air was neither long nor short, but just enough to grip,
Like yer own gets down yer collar, just before you gets a clip.

An' 'is tail was long and feth'ry, an' it give a sort of flirt,
An' 'is feet was rather large for 'im – but 'andy in the dirt,
An' 'is 'ide was odiferous – like lots of our 'ides were,
But the puppy couldn't 'elp it, so o' course 'e didn't care.

'Ow *could* 'e 'elp the reek and mud an' scavenging an' mice?
But you loved 'im all the same for that, 'is manners was so nice;
An' 'e always slep' inside my arm, 'is nose shoved in my ear,
An' although 'is breath did stink o' rats, it weren't as bad as beer.

But one evenin' 'e was sick of rats an' fancied somethin' more,
An' 'e slid out in the darkness through the narrow dug-out door,

An' there came a blinkin' German shell – which ain't no merry jest
An' it scattered, like the blazin' 'ell – an' Davy, 'e went West.

I crep' out in the open, tho' I knew I'd broke a rule,
And the other chaps they cursed me for a bloomin' silly fool,
But I brought 'is little body in – I couldn't leave it there,
Just 'is little yellow body with the soft fine yellow 'air.

Well, it's just as well it 'appened, for I couldn't 'a brought 'im 'ome,
All the other dogs 'd laugh at 'im – 'e's better in the loam,
An' I know 'e's quiet an' 'appy, in 'is native Flanders clay,
An' 'e might 'ave only fretted down in Mare Street, 'Ackney way.

But 'is spirit's often with me – for you never *lose* a friend –
Nosin' rats just round the corner, and 'e'll meet you at the bend,
An' we likes each other's comp'ny – when I'm sleepin' like a log,
I can feel a friendly snufflin' an' the 'appy smell of dog.

Dogs of Fear

Dante (c. 1265–1321), anonymous nineteenth-century translation

From *Inferno*

Here Cerberus, a strange and cruel beast,
Barks dog-like with his triple throat
Over the spirits in the swamp immersed.
He has vermilion eyes, a black and oily beard,
a monstrous belly, and his hands are clawed.
Clutching the souls, he skins and teareth them.
Beneath the rain like curs they howl
With one the other side to shield,
often they turn those wretched souls profane.

When he saw us, that huge worm, Cerberus,
opened his mouths and showed his tusks,
quivering the while through every limb.

Thearat my Guide spread out his hands
and took up earth, which from full fists
he straight into those greedy gullets flung.

Then, as a dog which in his hunger howls
is pacified soon as he bites his food, –
struggling and striving but to glut his maw, –
so stilled were those foul faces of
the demon Cerberus, whose wont it is
to thunder till the souls would willingly be deaf.

Canto VI, lines 13 to 33

Charlotte Brontë (1816–1855)

From *Jane Eyre*

The din was on the causeway: a horse was coming; the windings
of the lane yet hid it, but it approached. I was just leaving the stile;
yet, as the path was narrow, I sat still to let it go by. In those days
I was young, and all sorts of fancies bright and dark tenanted my
mind: the memories of nursery stories were there amongst other
rubbish; and when they recurred, maturing youth added to them
a vigour and vividness beyond what childhood could give. As this
horse approached, and as I watched for it to appear through the
dusk, I remembered certain of Bessie's tales, wherein figured a North-
of-England spirit called a 'Gytrash', which, in the form of horse, mule
or large dog, haunted solitary ways, and sometimes came upon
belated travellers, as this horse was now coming upon me.

It was very near, but not yet in sight; when, in addition to the
tramp, tramp, I heard a rush under the hedge,
and close down by the hazel stems glided a
great dog, whose black and white colour
made him a distinct object against
the trees. It was exactly one form of
Bessie's Gytrash – a lion-like creature
with long hair and a huge head: it
passed me, however, quietly enough;
not staying to look up, with strange
pretercanine eyes, in my face, as I
half expected it would. The horse
followed, – a tall steed, and on its back
a rider. The man, the human being,
broke the spell at once. Nothing ever

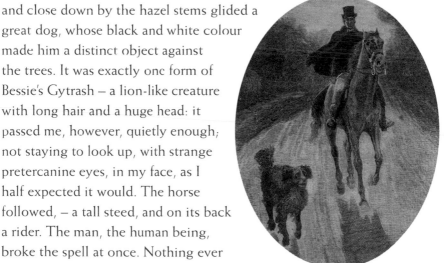

rode the Gytrash: it was always alone; and goblins, to my notions, though they might tenant the dumb carcasses of beasts, could scarce covet shelter in the commonplace human form. No Gytrash was this, – only a traveller taking the short cut to Millcote. He passed, and I went on; a few steps, and I turned: a sliding sound and an exclamation of 'What the deuce is to do now?' and a clattering tumble, arrested my attention. Man and horse were down; they had slipped on the sheet of ice which glazed the causeway. The dog came bounding back, and seeing his master in a predicament, and hearing the horse groan, barked till the evening hills echoed the sound, which was deep in proportion to his magnitude. He snuffed round the prostrate group, and then he ran up to me; it was all he could do, – there was no other help at hand to summon. I obeyed him, and walked down to the traveller, by this time struggling himself free of his steed. His efforts were so vigorous, I thought he could not be much hurt; but I asked him the question –

'Are you injured, sir?'

I think he was swearing, but am not certain; however, he was pronouncing some formula which prevented him from replying to me directly.

'Can I do anything?' I asked again.

'You must just stand on one side,' he answered as he rose, first to his knees, and then to his feet. I did; whereupon began a heaving, stamping, clattering process, accompanied by a barking and baying which removed me effectually some yards' distance; but I would not be driven quite away till I saw the event. This was finally fortunate; the horse was re-established, and the dog was silenced with a 'Down, Pilot!' The traveller now, stooping, felt his foot and leg, as if trying whether they were sound; apparently something ailed them, for he halted to the stile whence I had just risen, and sat down.

Charles Dickens (1812–1870)

From *Oliver Twist*

A white shaggy dog, with his face scratched and torn in twenty
different places, skulked into the room.

'Why didn't you come in afore?' said the man. 'You're getting too
proud to own me afore company, are you? Lie down!'

This command was accompanied with a kick, which sent the
animal to the other end of the room. He appeared well used to it,
however; for he coiled himself up in a corner very quietly, without
uttering a sound, and winking his very ill-looking eyes twenty
times in a minute, appeared to occupy himself in taking a survey of
the apartment.

There was a long pause. Every member of the respectable coterie
appeared plunged in his own reflections, not excepting the dog,
who by a certain malicious licking of
his lips seemed to be meditating
an attack upon the legs of
the first gentleman or lady
he might encounter in
the streets when he
went out.

Sir Arthur Conan Doyle (1859–1930)

From *The Hound of the Baskervilles*

Every minute that white woolly plain which covered one half
of the moor was drifting closer and closer to the house. Already
the first thin wisps of it were curling across the golden square of
the lighted window. The farther wall of the orchard was already
invisible, and the trees were standing out of a swirl of white vapour.
As we watched it the fog-wreaths came crawling round both
corners of the house and rolled slowly into one dense bank, on
which the upper floor and the roof floated like a strange ship upon
a shadowy sea. Holmes struck his hand passionately upon the rock
in front of us, and stamped his feet in his impatience.

'If he isn't out in a quarter of an hour the path will be covered. In
half an hour we won't be able to see our hands in front of us.'

'Shall we move farther back upon higher ground?'

'Yes, I think it would be as well.'

So as the fog-bank flowed onwards we fell back before it until we
were half a mile from the house, and still that dense white sea, with
the moon silvering its upper edge, swept slowly and inexorably on.

'We are going too far,' said Holmes, 'We dare not take the chance
of his being overtaken before he can reach us. At all costs we must
hold our ground where we are.' He dropped on his knees and clapped
his ear to the ground. 'Thank God, I think that I hear him coming.'

A sound of quick steps broke the silence of the moor. Crouching
among the stones, we stared intently at the silver-tipped bank in
front of us. The steps grew louder, and through the fog, as through
a curtain, there stepped the man whom we were awaiting. He
looked round him in surprise as he emerged into the clear, star-lit
night. Then he came swiftly along the path, passed close to where

we lay, and went on up the long
slope behind us. As he walked he
glanced continually over either
shoulder, like a man who is ill
at ease.

'Hist!' cried Holmes, and
I heard the sharp click of a
cocking pistol. 'Look out! It's
coming!'

There was a thin, crisp, continuous
patter from somewhere in the heart of
that crawling bank. The cloud was within fifty yards of where
we lay, and we glared at it, all three, uncertain what horror was
about to break from the heart of it. I was at Holmes's elbow, and
I glanced for an instant at his face. It was pale and exultant, his
eyes shining brightly in the moonlight. But suddenly they started
forward in a rigid, fixed stare, and his lips parted in amazement. At
the same instant Lestrade gave a yell of terror and threw himself
face downwards upon the ground. I sprang to my feet, my inert
hand grasping my pistol, my mind paralysed by the dreadful shape
which had sprung upon us from the shadows of the fog. A hound
it was, an enormous coal-black hound, but not such a hound as
mortal eyes have ever seen. Fire burst from its open mouth, its
eyes glowed with a smouldering glare, its muzzle and hackles and
dewlap were outlined in flickering flame. Never in the delirious
dream of a disordered brain could anything more savage, more
appalling, more hellish, be conceived than that dark form and
savage face which broke upon us out of the wall of fog.

With long bounds the huge black creature was leaping down
the track, following hard upon the footsteps of our friend. So
paralysed were we by the apparition that we allowed him to pass

before we had recovered our nerve. The Holmes and I both fired together, and the creature gave a hideous howl, which showed that one at least had hit him. He did not pause, however, but bounded onwards. Far away on the path we saw Sir Henry looking back, his face white in the moonlight, his hands raised in horror, glaring helplessly at the frightful thing which was hunting him down.

But that cry of pain from the hound had blown all our fears to the winds. If he was vulnerable he was mortal, and if we could wound him we could kill him. Never have I seen a man run as Holmes ran that night. I am reckoned fleet of foot, but he outpaced me as much as I outpaced the little professional. In front of us as we flew up the track we heard scream after scream from Sir Henry and the deep roar of the hound. I was in time to see the beast spring upon its victim, hurl him to the ground and worry at his throat. But the next instant Holmes had emptied five barrels of his revolver into the creature's flank. With a last howl of agony and a vicious snap in the air it rolled upon its back, four feet pawing furiously, and then fell limp upon its side. I stooped, panting, and pressed my pistol to the dreadful, shimmering head, but it was useless to press the trigger. The giant hound was dead.

Ray Bradbury (1920–2012)

The Emissary

Martin knew it was autumn again, for Dog ran into the house bringing wind and frost and a smell of apples turned to cider under trees. In dark clocksprings of hair, Dog fetched goldenrod, dust of farewell-summer, acorn-husk, hair of squirrel, feather of departed robin, sawdust from fresh-cut cordwood, and leaves like charcoals shaken from a blaze of maple trees. Dog jumped. Showers of brittle fern, blackberry vine, marsh grass sprang over the bed where Martin shouted. No doubt, no doubt of it at all, this incredible beast was October!

'Here, boy, here!'

And Dog settled to warm Martin's body with all the bonfires and subtle burnings of the season, to fill the room with soft or heavy, wet or dry odors of far-traveling. In spring, he smelled of lilac, iris, lawn-mowered grass; in summer, ice-cream-mustached, he came pungent with firecracker, Roman candle, pinwheel, baked by the sun. But autumn! Autumn!

'Dog, what's it like outside?'

And lying there, Dog told as he always told. Lying there, Martin found autumn as in the old days before sickness bleached him white on his bed. Here was his contact, his carryall, the quick-moving part of himself he sent with a yell to run and return, circle and scent, collect and deliver the time and texture of worlds in town, country, by creek, river, lake, down-cellar, up-attic, in closet or coalbin. Ten dozen times a day he was gifted with sunflower seed, cinder-path, milkweed, horse chestnut or full flame smell of pumpkin. Through the looming of the universe Dog shuttled; the design was hid in *his* pelt. Put our your hand, it was there ...

'And where did you go this morning?'

But he knew without hearing where Dog had rattled down hills where autumn lay in cereal crispness, where children lay in funeral pyres, in rustling heaps, the leaf-buried but watchful dead, as Dog and the world blew by. Martin trembled his fingers, searched the thick fur, read the long journey. Through stubbled fields, over glitters of ravine creek, down marbled spread of cemetery yard, into woods. In the great season of spices and rare incense, now

Martin ran through his emissary, around, about and home!

The bedroom door opened.

'That dog of yours is in trouble again.'

Mother brought in a tray of fruit salad, cocoa and toast, her blue eyes snapping.

'Mother .. .'

'Always digging places. Dug a hole in Miss Tarkins's garden this morning. She's spittin' mad. That's the fourth hole he's dug there this week.'

'Maybe he's looking for something.'

'Fiddlesticks, he's too darned curious. If he doesn't behave he'll be locked up.'

Martin looked at this woman as if she were a stranger.

'Oh, you wouldn't do that! How would I learn anything? How would I find things out if Dog didn't tell me?'

Mom's voice was quieter. 'Is that what he does – tell you things?'

'There's nothing I don't know when he goes out and around and back, *nothing* I can't find out from him! '

They both sat looking at Dog and the dry strewings of mold and seed over the quilt.

'Well, if he'll just stop digging where he shouldn't, he can run all he wants,' said Mother.

'Here, boy, here!'

And Martin snapped a tin note to the dog's collar:

MY OWNER IS MARTIN SMITH
TEN YEARS OLD
SICK IN BED
VISITORS WELCOME.

Dog barked. Mother opened the downstairs door and let him out.

Martin sat listening.

Far off and away you could hear Dog run in the quiet autumn rain that was falling now. You could hear the barking-jingling fade, rise, fade again as he cut down alley, over lawn, to fetch back Mr Holloway and the oiled metallic smell of the delicate snowflake-interiored watches he repaired in his home shop. Or maybe he would bring Mr Jacobs, the grocer, whose clothes were rich with lettuce, celery, tomatoes and the secret tinned and hidden smell of the red demons stamped on cans of deviled ham. Mr Jacobs and his unseen pink-meat devils waved often from the yard below. Or Dog brought Mr Jackson, Mrs Gillespie, Mr Smith, Mrs Holmes, *any* friend or near-friend, encountered, cornered, begged, worried and at last shepherded home for lunch, or tea and biscuits.

Now, listening, Martin heard Dog below, with footsteps moving in a light rain behind him. The downstairs bell rang.

Mom opened the door, light voices murmured. Martin sat forward, face shining. The stair treads creaked. A young woman's voice laughed quietly. Miss Haight, of course, his teacher from school!

The bedroom door sprang open.

Martin had company.

Morning, afternoon, evening, dawn and dusk, sun and moon circled with Dog, who faithfully reported temperatures of turf and air, color of earth and tree, consistency of mist or rain, but – most important of all – brought back again and again and again – Miss Haight.

On Saturday, Sunday and Monday she baked Martin orange-iced cup-cakes, brought him library books about dinosaurs and cavemen. On Tuesday, Wednesday and Thursday somehow he beat her at dominoes, somehow she lost at checkers and soon, she cried, he'd defeat her handsomely at chess. On Friday, Saturday and Sunday they talked and never stopped talking, and she was *so* young and laughing and handsome and her hair was a soft, shining brown like the season outside the window, and she walked dear, clean and quick, a heartbeat warm in the bitter afternoon when he heard it. Above all, she had the secret of signs, and could read and interpret Dog and the symbols she searched out and plucked forth from his coat with her miraculous fingers. Eyes shut, softly laughing, in a gypsy's voice, she divined the world from the treasure in her hands.

And on Monday afternoon, Miss Haight was dead.

Martin sat up in bed, slowly.

'Dead?' he whispered.

Dead, said his mother, yes, dead, killed in an auto accident a mile out of town. Dead, yes, dead, which meant cold to Martin, which meant silence and whiteness and winter come long before its time. Dead, silent, cold, white. The thoughts circled round, blew down and settled in whispers.

Martin held Dog, thinking; turned to the wall. The lady with the autumn-colored hair. The lady with the laughter that was very gentle and never made fun and the eyes that watched your mouth to see everything you ever said. The other-half-of-autumn-lady, who told what was left untold by Dog, about the world. The heartbeat at the still center of gray afternoon. The heartbeat fading ...

'Mom? What do they do in the graveyard, Mom, under the ground? Just lay there?'

'*Lie* there.'

'Lie there? Is that *all* they do? It doesn't sound like much fun.'

'For goodness' sake, it's not made out to be fun.'

'Why don't they jump up and run around once in a while if they get tired of lying there? God's pretty silly – '

'Martin!'

'Well, you'd think He'd treat people better than to tell them to
lie still for keeps. That's impossible. Nobody can do it! I tried once.
Dog tries. I tell him, 'Dead Dog!" He plays dead awhile, then gets
sick and tired and wags his tail or opens one eye and looks at me,
bored. Boy, I bet sometimes those graveyard people do the same,
huh, Dog?'

Dog barked.

'Be still with that kind of talk!' said Mother.

Martin looked off into space.

'Bet that's exactly what they do,' he said.

Autumn burned the trees bare and ran Dog still farther around,
fording creek, prowling graveyard as was his custom, and back in
the dusk to fire off volleys of barking that shook windows wherever
he turned.

In the late last days of October, Dog began to act as if the wind
had changed and blew from a strange country. He stood quivering
on the porch below. He whined, his eyes fixed at the empty land
beyond town. He brought no visitors for Martin. He stood for
hours each day, as if leashed, trembling, then shot away straight,
as if someone had called. Each night he returned later, with no one
following. Each night, Martin sank deeper and deeper in his pillow.

'Well, people are busy,' said Mother. 'They haven't time to notice
the tag Dog carries. Or they mean to come visit, but forget.'

But there was more to it than that. There was the fevered shining
in Dog's eyes, and his whimpering tic late at night, in some private
dream. His shivering in the dark, under the bed. The way he
sometimes stood half the night, looking at Martin as if some
great and impossible secret was his and he knew no way to tell it
save by savagely thumping his tail, or turning in endless circles,

never to lie down, spinning and spinning again.

On October 30, Dog ran out and didn't come back at all, even when after supper Martin heard his parents call and call.

The hour grew late, the streets and sidewalks stood empty, the air moved cold about the house, and there was nothing, nothing.

Long after midnight, Martin lay watching the world beyond the cool, clear glass windows. Now there was not even autumn, for there was no Dog to fetch it in. There would be no winter, for who could bring the snow to melt in your hands? Father, Mother? No, not the same. They couldn't play the game with its special secrets and rules, its sounds and pantomimes. No more seasons. No more time. The go-between, the emissary, was lost to the wild throngings of civilization, poisoned, stolen, hit by a car, left somewhere in a culvert....

Sobbing, Martin turned his face to his pillow. The world was a picture under glass, untouchable. The world was dead.

Martin twisted in bed and in three days the last Halloween pumpkins were rotting in trash cans, papier-mache skulls and witches were burnt on bonfires, and ghosts were stacked on shelves with other linens until next year.

To Martin, Halloween had been nothing more than one evening when tin horns cried off in the cold autumn stars, children blew like goblin leaves along the flinty walks, flinging their heads, or cabbages, at porches, soap-writing names or similar magic symbols on icy windows. All of it as distant, unfathomable and nightmarish as a puppet show seen from so many miles away that there is no sound or meaning.

For three days in November, Martin watched alternate light and shadow sift across his ceiling. The fire pageant was over forever; autumn lay in cold ashes. Martin sank deeper, yet deeper in white marble layers of bed, motionless, listening, always listening …

Friday evening, his parents kissed him good night and walked out of the house into the hushed cathedral weather toward a motion-picture show. Miss Tarkins from next door stayed on in the parlor below until Martin called down he was sleepy, then took her knitting off home.

In silence, Martin lay following the great move of stars down a clear and moonlit sky, remembering nights such as this when he'd spanned the town with Dog ahead, behind, around about, cracking the green-plush ravine, lapping slumbrous streams gone milky with the fullness of the moon, leaping cemetery tombstones while whispering the marble names; on, quickly on, through shaved meadows where the only motion was the off-on quivering of stars, to streets where shadows would not stand aside for you but crowded all the sidewalks for mile on mile. Run, now, run! Chasing, being chased by bitter smoke, fog, mist, wind, ghost of mind, fright of memory; home, safe, sound, snug-warm, asleep …

Nine o'clock.

Chime. The drowsy clock in the deep stairwell below.

Chime.

Dog, come home, and run the world with you. Dog, bring a thistle with frost on it, or bring nothing else but the wind.

Dog, where *are* you? Oh, listen now, I'll call.

Martin held his breath.

Way off somewhere – a sound.

Martin rose up, trembling.

There, again – the sound.

So small a sound, like a sharp needle-point brushing the sky long miles and many miles away. The dreamy echo of a dog – barking.

The sounds of a dog crossing fields and farms, dirt roads and rabbit paths, running, running, letting out great barks of steam, cracking the night. The sound of a circling dog which came and went, lifted and faded, opened up, shut in, moved forward, went back, as if the animal were kept by someone on a fantastically long chain. As if the dog were running and someone whistled under the chestnut trees, in mold-shadow, tar-shadow, moon-shadow, walking, and the dog circled back and sprang our again toward home.

Dog! Martin thought. Oh, Dog, come home, boy! Listen, oh, listen, where have you *been?* Come on, boy, make tracks!

Five, ten, fifteen minutes; near, very near, the bark, the sound. Martin cried out, thrust his feet from the bed, leaned to the window. Dog! Listen, boy! Dog! Dog! He said it over and over. Dog! Dog! Wicked Dog, run off and gone all these days! Bad Dog, good Dog, home, boy, hurry, and bring what you can!

Near now, near, up the street, barking, to knock clapboard housefronts with sound, whirl iron cocks on rooftops in the moon, firing of volleys – Dog! now at the door below …

Martin shivered.

Should he run – let Dog in, or wait for Mom and Dad? Wait? Oh, God, wait? But what if Dog ran off again? No, he'd go down, snatch the door wide, yell, grab Dog in, and run upstairs so fast, laughing, crying, holding tight, that …

Dog stopped barking.

Hey! Martin almost broke the window, jerking to it.

Silence. As if someone had told Dog to hush now, hush, hush.

A full minute passed. Martin clenched his fists.

Below, a faint whimpering.

Then, slowly, the downstairs front door opened. Someone was kind enough to have opened the door for Dog. Of course! Dog had brought Mr Jacobs or Mr Gillespie or Miss Tarkins, or …

The downstairs door shut.

Dog raced upstairs, whining, flung himself on the bed.

'Dog, Dog, where've you *been*, what've you *done!* Dog, Dog!'

And he crushed Dog hard and long to himself, weeping, Dog, Dog. He laughed and shouted. Dog! But after a moment he stopped laughing and crying, suddenly.

He pulled back away. He held the animal and looked at him, eyes widening.

The odor coming from Dog was different.

It was a smell of strange earth. It was a smell of night within night, the smell of digging down deep in shadow through earth that had lain cheek by jowl with things that were long hidden and decayed. A stinking and rancid soil fell away in clods of dissolution from Dog's muzzle and paws.

He had dug deep. He had dug very deep indeed. That *was* it, wasn't it? Wasn't it? *Wasn't* it?

What kind of message was this from Dog? What could such a message mean? The stench – the ripe and awful cemetery earth.

Dog was a very bad dog, digging where he shouldn't. Dog was a good dog, always making friends. Dog loved people.

Dog brought them home.

And now, moving up the dark hall stairs, at intervals, came the sound of feet, one foot dragged after the other, painfully, slowly, slowly, slowly.

Dog shivered. A rain of strange night earth fell seething on the bed.

Dog turned.

The bedroom door whispered in.

Martin had company.

The Good
Companions

———

Harold Monro (1879–1932)

Dog

You little friend, your nose is ready; you sniff,
Asking for that expected walk,
(Your nostrils full of the happy rabbit-whiff)
And almost talk.

And so the moment becomes a moving force;
Coats glide down from their pegs in the humble dark;
The sticks grow live to the stride of their vagrant course.
You scamper the stairs,
Your body informed with the scent and the track and the mark
Of stoats and weasels, moles and badgers and hares.

We are going OUT. You know the pitch of the word,
Probing the tone of thought as it comes through fog
And reaches by devious means (half-smelt, half-heard)
The four-legged brain of a walk-ecstatic dog.

Out in the garden your head is already low.
(Can you smell the rose? Ah, no.)
But your limbs can draw
Life from the earth through the touch of your padded paw.

Now, sending a little look to us behind,
Who follow slowly the track of your lovely play,
You carry our bodies forward away from mind
Into the light and fun of your useless day.

* * * * *

Thus, for your walk, we took ourselves, and went
Out by the hedge and the tree to the open ground.
You ran, in delightful strata of wafted scent,
Over the hill without seeing the view;
Beauty is smell upon primitive smell to you:
To you, as to us, it is distant and rarely found.

Home … and further joy will be surely there:
Supper waiting full of the taste of bone.
You throw up your nose again, and sniff, and stare
For the rapture known
Of the quick wild gorge of food and the still lie-down
While your people talk above you in the light
Of candles, and your dreams will merge and drown
Into the bed-delicious hours of night.

Jerome K. Jerome (1859–1927)

From *Idle Thoughts of an Idle Fellow*

They [dogs] are much superior to human beings as companions.
They do not quarrel or argue with you. They never talk about
themselves, but listen to you while you talk about yourself, and
keep up an appearance of being interested in the conversation.
They never make stupid remarks. They never observe to Miss
Brown across a dinner-table that they always understood she was
very sweet on Mr. Jones (who has just married Miss Robinson).

They never mistake your wife's cousin for her husband, and fancy that you are the father-in-law.

And they never ask a young author with fourteen tragedies, sixteen comedies, seven farces and a couple of burlesques in his desk, why he doesn't write a play.

They never say unkind things. They never tell us of our faults, 'merely for our own good'. They do not, at inconvenient moments, mildly remind us of our past follies and mistakes. They do not say, 'Oh yes, a lot of use you are, if you are ever really wanted – ' sarcastic like. They never inform us, like our *inamoratas* sometimes do, that we are not nearly so nice as we used to be.

We are always the same to them.

Oliver Herford (1863–1935)

The Dog

The Dog is black, or white, or brown
　And sometimes spotted like a clown.
He loves to make a foolish noise
　And Human Company enjoys.

The Human People pat his head
　And teach him to pretend he's dead,
And beg, and fetch and carry too;
　Things that no well-bred Cat will do.

At Human jokes, however stale,
　He jumps about and wags his tail,

And Human People clap their hands
  And think he really understands.

They say 'Good Dog' to him. To us
  They say 'Poor Puss' and make no fuss.
Why Dogs are 'good' and Cats are 'poor'
  I fail to understand, I'm sure.

To Someone very Good and Just,
  Who has proved worthy of her trust,
A Cat will sometimes condescend –
  The Dog is Everybody's friend.

Leigh Hunt (1784–1859)

Human Qualities

One of the animals which a generous and sociable man would
soonest become is a dog. A dog can have a friend; he has affections
and character, he can equally enjoy the field and the fireside;
he dreams, he caresses, he propitiates; he offends and is pardoned;
he stands by you in adversity; he is a good fellow.

Anonymous

The dog is the only animal who has seen his god.

Charlotte Brontë (1816–1855)

From *Jane Eyre*

'I don't think he will see you," she answered; 'he refuses everybody.'

When she returned, I inquired what he had said. 'You are to send in your name and your business,' she replied. She then proceeded to fill a glass with water, and place it on a tray, together with candles.

'Is that what he rang for?' I asked.

'Yes: he always has candles brought in at dark, though he is blind."

'Give the tray to me; I will carry it in.'

I took it from her hand: she pointed me out the parlour door. The tray shook as I held it; the water spilt from the glass; my heart struck my ribs loud and fast. Mary opened the door for me, and shut it behind me.

This parlour looked gloomy: a neglected handful of fire burnt low in the grate; and, leaning over it, with his head supported against the high, old-fashioned mantelpiece, appeared the blind tenant of the room. His old dog, Pilot, lay on one side, removed out of the way, and coiled up as if afraid of being inadvertently trodden upon. Pilot pricked up his ears when I came in: then he jumped up with a yelp and a whine, and bounded towards me: he almost knocked the tray from my hands. I set it on the table; then patted him, and said softly, 'Lie down!' Mr. Rochester turned mechanically to see what the commotion was: but as he saw nothing, he returned and sighed.

'Give me the water, Mary,' he said.

I approached him with the now only half-filled glass; Pilot followed me, still excited.

'What is the matter?" he inquired.

'Down, Pilot!' I again said. He checked the water on its way to his lips, and seemed to listen: he drank, and put the glass down. 'This is you, Mary, is it not?'

'Mary is in the kitchen,' I answered.

He put out his hand with a quick gesture, but not seeing where I stood, he did not touch me. 'Who is this? Who is this?' he demanded, trying, as it seemed, to see with those sightless eyes – unavailing and distressing attempt! 'Answer me – speak again!' he ordered, imperiously and aloud.

'Will you have a little more water, sir? I spilt half of what was in the glass,' I said.

'Who is it? What is it? Who speaks?'

'Pilot knows me, and John and Mary know I am here. I came only this evening,' I answered.

'Great God! – what delusion has come over me? What sweet madness has seized me?'

'No delusion – no madness: your mind, sir, is too strong for delusion, your health too sound for frenzy.'

'And where is the speaker? Is it only a voice? Oh! I cannot see, but I must feel, or my heart will stop and my brain burst. Whatever – whoever you are – be perceptible to the touch or I cannot live!'

Sir Walter Scott (1771–1832)

The misery of keeping a dog is his dying so soon; but to be sure if he lived for fifty years, *and then died*, what would become of me?

Emile Zola (1840–1902)

From *Why I Love My Dog*

I had a little dog, a griffon of the smallest kind, whose name was *Fanfan*. One day, at the dog show at Cours-la-Reine, I saw him in a cage, with a large cat as a companion. He regarded me with eyes so full of sadness that I asked the attendant to let him out of his cage for a little while. As soon as he was on the ground he commenced to walk like a little toy dog. Enthusiastically I bought him. It was a little mad dog. One morning, after I had him about a week, he commenced to turn in a circle without ceasing, round and round without ever stopping. When he had fallen with fatigue, in appearance drunk, he would painfully raise himself and set to turning again. When, seized by pity, I took him in my arms, his paws would keep up the movement of the continual round, and when I placed him on the ground, he commenced turning again, turning always. I called in a veterinary, who spoke of an injury to the brain. Then he offered to poison him. I refused. All the animals who live with me die a natural death, and they all sleep in a tranquil corner of my garden. *Fanfan* appeared recovered after this first attack. During the two years that it entered into my life, it was so much to me that I cannot find words to describe it. It never quitted me, crouching near to me, in the bottom of my armchair, in the morning during my four hours of work; it had become, thus, part of my agony, part of my joys, raising its little nose at the moments of repose, and regarding me with its little clear eyes. And then it took part in all my walks, going before me with his gait of little toy dog, which used to make all the passers-by laugh, sleeping, when we returned, under my chair, passing the night upon a cushion at the foot of my bed. There was a tie so strong between us that, even at the shortest of separations, I missed him as much as he missed me.

And shortly *Fanfan* became again mad. He had two or three attacks at different intervals. Then the attacks were so frequent that our life was frightful. When the madness was upon him, he would turn and turn without ceasing. I was not able to keep him in my chair. A demon seemed to possess him. And I have seen him turn for two hours around my table. But it was in the night that I suffered the most, hearing him do this involuntary round, head-strong and savage, with the continual noise of the fall of his little paws upon the carpet. I have often risen and taken him in my arms, keeping him thus for an hour, two hours, hoping that the attack would subside, but as soon as I put him to the ground he would commence to turn.

People laughed at me, and said I was mad myself to keep the dog in my room. I could not do otherwise. My heart melted at the idea that I should not be there any more to take him and try to calm him, and that he would regard me no more, with his little clear eyes, his eyes distracted by misery, yet which thanked me.

It was thus, in my arms, one morning, that *Fanfan* died while regarding me. He had but a slight shock, and all was finished. I felt simply his little convulsed body become of the suppleness of chiffon. The tears came to my eyes, and I felt it was a loss to me. An animal, nothing but a little animal, and to suffer thus at its loss! To be haunted by its recollection to such an extent, that I wished to write of my sorrow, certain of leaving the impression of my heart on the page! To-day, all that is distant, and other sorrows have come, and I feel that the things I have said are cold. But then it seemed to me that I had so much to say, that I should have said the things profound, definite, upon this love of animals – so obscure and so powerful, at which I see people around me smile, and which pains me to the extent of troubling my life.

And why was I attached so profoundly to this little mad dog?
Why have I fraternised with it as one fraternises with a human
being? Why have I cried as one cries for a lost friend? Is it not
that the unquenchable tenderness which I feel for everything
which lives and feels is a brotherhood of suffering! a charity which
inclines one towards the most humble and disinherited.

Geoffrey Chaucer (1343–1400)

From *The General Prologue to The Canterbury Tales*

There was also a Nonne, a Prioresse,
Of smale houndes hadde she that she fedde
With rosted flesh, or milk and wastel-breed.
But soore wepte she if oon of hem were deed,
Or if men smoot it with a yerde smerte;
And al was conscience and tender herte.

Charles Dickens (1812–1870)

From *David Copperfield*

'You are not very intimate with Miss Murdstone, are you?' said
Doran. 'My pet.' (The last two words were to the dog. Oh if they
had only been to me!)
    'No,' I replied, 'Not at all so.'

'She is a tiresome creature,' said Dora, pouting. 'Who wants a protector? I am sure I don't want a protector. Jip can protect me a great deal better than Miss Murdstone, – can't you, Jip, dear?'

He only winked lazily, when she kissed his ball of a head.

'Papa calls her my confidential friend, but I am sure she is no such thing – is she Jip. We are not going to confide in any such cross people, Jip and I. We mean to bestow our confidences where we like, and to find out our own friends, instead of having them found for us – don't we Jip?'

Jip made a comfortable noise, in answer, a little like a tea-kettle when it sings.

Elizabeth Barrett Browning (1806–1861)

Flush or Faunus

You see this dog. It was but yesterday
I mused forgetful of his presence here
Till thought on thought drew downward tear on tear,
When from the pillow, where wet-cheeked I lay,
A head as hairy as Faunus thrust its way
Right sudden against my face – two golden-clear
Great eyes astonished mine, – a drooping ear
Did flap me on either cheek to dry the spray!
I started first, as some Arcadian,
Amazed by goatly god in twilight grove;
But, as the bearded vision closelier ran
My tears off, I knew Flush, and rose above
Surprise and sadness – thanking the true Pan,
Who, by low creatures, leads to heights of love.

Virginia Woolf (1882–1941)

From *Flush: A Biography*

Then such a wave of despair and
anguish overwhelmed him, the
irrevocableness and implacability
of fate so smote him, that he lifted
up his head and howled aloud. A
voice said 'Flush'. He did not hear
it. 'Flush,' it repeated a second time.
He started. He had thought himself
alone. He turned. Was there something
alive in the room with him? Was there
something on the sofa? In the wild hope that

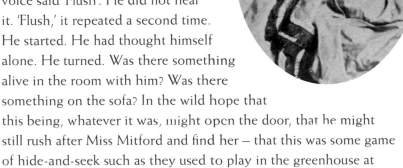

this being, whatever it was, might open the door, that he might
still rush after Miss Mitford and find her – that this was some game
of hide-and-seek such as they used to play in the greenhouse at
home – Flush darted to the sofa.

'Oh, Flush!' said Miss Barrett. For the first time she looked him in
the face. For the first time Flush looked at the lady lying on the sofa.
Each was surprised. Heavy curls hung down on either side of
Miss Barrett's face; large bright eyes shone out; a large mouth
smiled. Heavy ears hung down on either side of Flush's face; his
eyes, too, were large and bright; his mouth was wide. There was
a likeness between them. As they gazed at each other each felt:
Here am I – and then each felt: But how different! Hers was the
pale worn face of an invalid, cut off from air, light, freedom. His
was the warm ruddy face of a young animal; instinct with health
and energy. Broken asunder, yet made in the same mould, could
it be that each completed what was dormant in the other? She

might have been – all that; and he – But no. Between them lay the widest gulf that can separate one being from another. She spoke. He was dumb. She was woman; he was dog. Thus closely united, thus immensely divided, they gazed at each other. Then with one bound Flush sprang on to the sofa and laid himself where he was to lie for ever after – on the rug at Miss Barrett's feet.

Eleanor Atkinson (1863–1942)

From *Greyfriars Bobby*

Bobby had slept blissfully nearly all the day, after his exhausting labours and torturing pains. But with the sunset bugle he fretted to be let out. Ailie had wept and pleaded, Mrs. Brown had reasoned with him and Mr. Brown had scolded, all to the end of persuading him to sleep in 'the hoose the nicht'. But when no-one was watching him Bobby crawled from his rug and dragged himself to the door. He rapped the floor with his tail in delight when Mr. Traill came in and bundled him up on the rug, so he could lie easily, and carried him down to the gate.

For quite twenty minutes these neighbours and friends of Bobby filed by silently, patted the shaggy little head, looked at the grand plate with Bobby's and the Lord Provost's names upon it, and believed their own wondering een. Bobby wagged his tail and lolled his tongue, and now and then he licked the hand of a baby who had to be lifted by a tall brother to see him. Shy kisses were dropped on Bobby's head by toddling bairns, and awkward caresses by rough laddies. Then they all went home quietly, and Mr. Traill carried the little dog around the kirk.

And there, ah! so belated, Auld Jock's grave bore its tribute of
flowers. Wreaths and nosegays, potted daffodils and primroses
and daisies, covered the sunken mound so that some of them had
to be moved to make room for Bobby. He sniffed and sniffed at
them, looked up inquiringly at Mr. Traill, and then snuggled down
contentedly among the blossoms. He did not understand their
being there any more than he understood the collar about which
everybody made such a to-do. The narrow band of leather would
disappear under his thatch again, and would be unnoticed by the
casual passer-by; the flowers would fade and never be so lavishly
renewed; but there was another more wonderful gift, now, that
would never fail him.

At nightfall, before the drum and bugle sounded the tattoo to
call the scattered garrison in the Castle, there took place a loving
ceremony that was never afterward omitted as long as Bobby lived.
Every child newly come to the tenements learned it, every weanie
lisped it among his first words. Before going to bed each bairn
opened a casement. Sometimes a candle was held up – a little star
of love, glimmering for a moment in the dark; but always there
was a small face peering into the melancholy
kirkyard. In midsummer, and at other
seasons if the moon rose full and early
and the sky was clear, Bobby could
be seen on the grave. And when he
recovered from these hurts he trotted
about, making the circuit below the
windows.

He could not speak there, because
he had been forbidden, but he could
wag his tail and look up to show his
friendliness. And whether the children

saw him or not, they knew he was always there after sunset,
keeping watch and ward, and 'lanely' because his master had gone
away to heaven; and so they called out to him sweetly and clearly:
  'A gude nicht to ye, Bobby.'

Frances Cornford (1886–1960)

A Child's Dream

I had a little dog, and my dog was very small
He licked me in the face and he answered to my call;
Of all the treasures that were mine, I loved him most of all.

His nose was fresh as morning dew and blacker than the night;
I thought that it could even snuff the shadows and the light;
And his tail he held bravely, like a banner in a fight.

His body covered thick with hair was very good to smell;
His little stomach underneath was pink as any shell;
And I loved him and I honoured him more than words can tell.

We ran out in the morning, both of us to play
Up and down across the fields for all the sunny day;
But he ran so swiftly – he ran right away.

I looked for him, I called him – entreatingly. Alas,
The dandelions could not speak, though they had seen him pass.
And nowhere was his waving tail among the waving grass.

I called him in a thousand ways and yet he did not come.
The pathways and the hedges were horrible and dumb.
I prayed to God who never heard. My desperate soul grew numb.

The sun sank low. I ran; I prayed; 'If God has not the power
To find him, let me die. I cannot bear another hour.'
When suddenly I came upon a great yellow flower.

And all among its petals, such was Heaven's grace,
In that golden hour, in that golden place
All among its petals, was his hairy face.

Algernon Charles Swinburne (1837–1909)

The Hound Hodain

But that same night in Cornwall oversea
Couched at Queen Iseult's hand, against her knee,
With keen kind eyes that read her whole heart's pain,
Fast at wide watch lay Tristram's hound Hodain,
The goodliest and the mightiest born on earth,
That many a forest day of fiery mirth
Had plied his craft between them; and the queen
Cherished him, even for those dim years between,
More than of old in those bright months far flown
When ere a blast of Tristram's horn was blown
Each morning as the woods rekindled, ere
Day gat full empire of the glimmering air,
Delight of sawn would quicken him. And fire

Spring and pant in his breath with bright desire
To be among the dewy ways on quest:
But now perforce at restless-hearted rest
He chafed through days more barren than the sand,
Soothed hardly, but soothed only with her hand,
Though fain to fawn thereon and follow, still
With all his heart and all his loving will
Desiring one divided from his sight,
For whose lost sake dawn was as dawn of night
And noon as night's noon in his eyes was dark.

And Iseult, worn with watch long held on pain,
Turned, and her eye lit on the hound Hodain,
And all her heart went out in tears: and he
Laid his kind head along her bended knee,
Till round his neck her arms went hard, and all
The night passed from her as a chain might fall:
But yet the heart within her, half undone,
Wailed, and was loth to let her see the sun.

From 'Tristram of Lyonesse'

Jack London (1876–1916)

From *Jerry of the Islands*

In the late afternoon, Jerry trotted aft, after having administered
another lesson to the wild-dog, and found Skipper seated on the
deck, back against the low rail, knees drawn up and gazing absently
off to leeward. Jerry sniffed his bare calf – not that he needed to

identify it, but just because he liked to, and in a sort of friendly greeting. But Van Horn took no notice, continuing to stare out across the sea. Nor was he aware of the puppy's presence.

Jerry rested the length of his chin on Skipper's knee and gazed long and earnestly into Skipper's face. This time Skipper knew, and was pleasantly thrilled; but still he gave no sign. Jerry tried a new tack. Skipper's hand drooped idly, half open, from where the forearm rested on the other knee. Into the part-open hand Jerry thrust his soft golden muzzle to the eyes and remained quite still. Had he been situated to see, he would have seen a twinkle in Skipper's eyes, which had been withdrawn from the sea and were looking down upon him. But Jerry could not see. He kept quiet a little longer, and then gave a prodigious sniff.

This was too much for Skipper, who laughed with such genial heartiness as to lay Jerry's silky ears back and down in self-deprecation of affection and pleadingness to bask in the sunshine of the god's smile. Also, Skipper's laughter set Jerry's tail wildly bobbing. The half-open hand closed in a firm grip that gathered in the slack of the skin of one side of Jerry's head and jowl. Then the hand began to shake him back and forth with such good will that he was compelled to balance back and forth on all his four feet.

It was bliss to Jerry. Nay, more, it was ecstasy. For Jerry knew there was neither anger nor danger in the roughness of the shake, and that it was play of the sort that he and Michael had indulged in. On occasion, he had so played with Biddy and lovingly mauled her about. And, on very rare occasion, Mister Haggin had lovingly mauled him about. It was speech to Jerry, full of unmistakable meaning.

As the shake grew rougher, Jerry emitted his most ferocious growl, which grew more ferocious with the increasing violence of the shaking. But that, too, was play, a making believe to hurt the one he liked too well to hurt. He strained and tugged at the grip, trying to twist his jowl in the slack of skin so as to reach a bite.

When Skipper, with a quick thrust, released him and shoved him clear, he came back, all teeth and growl, to be again caught and shaken. The play continued, with rising excitement to Jerry. Once, too quick for Skipper, he caught his hand between teeth; but he did not bring them together. They pressed lovingly, denting the skin, but there was no bite in them.

The play grew rougher, and Jerry lost himself in the play. Still playing, he grew so excited that all that had been feigned became actual. This was battle, a struggle against the hand that seized and shook him and thrust him away. The make-believe of ferocity passed out of his growls; the ferocity in them became real. Also, in the moments when he was shoved away and was springing back to the attack, he yelped in high-pitched puppy hysteria. And Captain Van Horn, realizing, suddenly, instead of clutching, extended his hand wide open in the peace sign that is as ancient as the human hand. At the same time his voice rang out the single word, 'Jerry!' In it was all the imperativeness of reproof and command and all the solicitous insistence of love.

Jerry knew and was checked back to himself. He was instantly contrite, all soft humility, ears laid back with pleadingness for forgiveness and protestation of a warm throbbing heart of love. Instantly, from an open-mouthed, fang-bristling dog in full career of attack, he melted into a bundle of softness and silkiness, that trotted to the open hand and kissed it with a tongue that flashed out between white gleaming teeth like a rose-red jewel. And the next moment he was in Skipper's arms, jowl against cheek, and the tongue was again flashing out in all the articulateness possible for a creature denied speech. It was a veritable love-feast, as dear to one as to the other.

'Gott-fer-dang!' Captain Van Horn crooned. 'You're nothing but a bunch of high-strung sensitiveness, with a golden heart in the middle and a golden coat wrapped all around. Gott-fer-dang, Jerry, you're gold, pure gold, inside and out, and no dog was ever minted like you in all the world. You're heart of gold, you golden dog, and be good to me and love me as I shall always be good to you and love you for ever and for ever.'

And Captain Van Horn, who ruled the Arangi in bare legs, a loin cloth and a sixpenny under-shirt, and ran cannibal blacks back and forth in the blackbird trade with an automatic strapped to his body waking and sleeping and with his head forfeit in scores of salt-water villages and bush strongholds, and who was esteemed the toughest skipper in the Solomons where only men who are tough may continue to live and esteem toughness, blinked with sudden moisture in his eyes, and could not see for the moment the puppy that quivered all its body of love in his arms and kissed away the salty softness of his eyes.

Lost Friends
———

Rudyard Kipling (1865–1936)

Four-Feet

I have done mostly what most men do,
And pushed it out of my mind;
But I can't forget, if I wanted to,
Four-Feet trotting behind.

Day after day, the whole day through –
Wherever my road inclined –
Four-Feet said, 'I am coming with you!'
And trotted along behind.

Now I must go by some other round, –
Which I shall never find –
Somewhere that does not carry the sound
Of Four-Feet trotting behind.

Lord Byron (1788–1824)

An Epitaph

EPITAPH ON HIS DOG, BURIED AT NEWSTEAD ABBEY
Near this spot
Are deposited the remains of one
Who possessed beauty without vanity,
Strength without insolence,
Courage without ferocity,

And all the virtues of man without his vices.
This praise, which would be unmeaning flattery
If inscribed over human ashes,
Is but a just tribute to the memory of
Boatswain, a dog.

Lord Byron (1788–1824)

Inscription on the Monument of a Newfoundland Dog

When some proud son of man returns to earth,
Unknown to glory, but upheld by birth,
The sculptor's art exhausts the pomp of woe
And storied urns record who rests below:
When all is done, upon the tomb is seen,
Not what he was, but what he should have been:
But the poor dog, in life the firmest friend,
The first to welcome, foremost to defend,
Whose honest heart is still his master's own,
Who labours, fights, lives, breathes for him alone,
Unhonour'd falls, unnoticed all his worth,
Denied in heaven the soul he held on earth:
While man, vain insect! hopes to be forgiven,
And claims himself a sole exclusive heaven.
Oh man! thou feeble tenant of an hour,
Debased by slavery, or corrupt by power,
Who knows thee well must quit thee with disgust,
Degraded mass of animated dust!

Thy love is lust, thy friendship all a cheat,
Thy smiles hypocrisy, thy words deceit!
By nature vile, ennobl'd but by name,
Each kindred brute might bid thee blush for shame.
Ye! who perchance behold this simple urn,
Pass on – it honours none who wish to mourn;
To mark a friend's remains these stones arise;
I never knew but one – and here he lies.

R. C. Lehmann (1856–1929)

A Retriever's Epitaph

Beneath this turf, that formerly he pressed
With agile feet, a dog is laid to rest.
Him as he sleeps no well-known sound shall stir,
The rabbits' patter or the pheasants whir;
The keeper's 'Over' – far, but well defined,
That speeds the startled partridge down the wind;
The whistled warning as the winged ones rise
Large and more large upon our straining eyes,
Till with a sweep while every nerve is tense
The chattering covey hurtles o'er the fence;
The double crack of every lifted gun;
The dinting thud of birds whose course is done; –
The sounds, delightful to the listening ear,
He heeds no longer, for he cannot hear.
None stauncher till the drive was done, defied
Temptation, rooted to his master's side;

None swifter, when his master gave the word,
Leapt on his course to track the running bird,
And bore it back – ah, many a time and oft!
His nose as faultless as his mouth was soft.
How consciously, how proudly unconcerned
Straight to his master's side he then returned,
Wagged a glad tail, and deemed himself repaid,
As in that master's hand that bird he laid,
If, while a word of praise was duly said,
The hand should stroke his smooth and honest head.
Through spring and summer in the sportless days
Cheerful he lived a life of simpler ways:
Chose, since official dogs at times unbend
The household cat for confidante and friend;
With children friendly, but untaught to fawn,
Romped through the walks and rollicked on the lawn,
Rejoiced if one the frequent ball should throw,
To fetch it, scampering gaily to and fro,
Content through every change of sportive mood
If one dear voice, one only, called him good.
Such was my dog, who now without my aid
Hunts through the Shadowland, himself a shade;
Or crouched intent before some ghostly gate,
Waits for my step, as here he used to wait.

Sir Arthur Conan Doyle (1859–1930)

To Carlo (Died July, 1921)

No truer, kinder soul
  Was ever sped than thine.
You lived without a growl,
  You died without a whine.

Rev. Sir George Ralph Fetherston (1784–1853)

Dedication

To the
Deathless Memory of my Dearest Friends,
companions in all my walks
and journeys,
true and loving in all their ways,
and deeply mourned in death!
DEAR FRITZ, MACK, PADDY, LAURIE
AND MANY OTHERS,
I Dedicate this Book,
believing that in the path of life,
no friend, however faithful, can be
more full of unselfish devotion,
at all times,
In Cloud or in Sunshine,
than
A DOG!

Jonathan Swift (1667–1745)

Epitaph

Of all the dogs arrayed in fur,
Hereunder lies the truest cur.
He knew no tricks, he never flattered:
Nor those he fawned upon bespattered.

W. H. Davies (1871–1940)

D for Dog

My dog went mad and bit my hand,
    I was bitten to the bone;
My wife went out walking with him
    And then came back alone.

I smoked my pipe, I nursed my wound,
    I saw them both depart;
But when my wife came back alone
    I was bitten to the heart.

Robert Burns (1759–1796)

On the Death of a Lap-Dog named Echo

In wood and wild, ye warbling throng,
  Your heavy loss deplore;
Now half-extinct your powers of song,
  Sweet Echo is no more.

Ye jarring, screeching things around,
  Scream your discordant joys;
Now half your din of tuneless sound
  With Echo silent lies.

Sir William Watson (1858–1935)

An Epitaph

His friends he loved. His fellest earthly foes –
Cats – I believe he did but feign to hate.
My hand will miss the insinuated nose,
Mine eyes the tail that wagg'd contempt at Fate.

Rudyard Kipling (1865–1936)

The Power of the Dog

There is sorrow enough in the natural way
From men and women to fill our day;
But when we are certain of sorrow in store,
Why do we always arrange for more?
Brothers and sisters, I bid you beware
Of giving your heart to a dog to tear.

Buy a pup and your money will buy
Love unflinching that cannot lie –
Perfect passion and worship fed
By a kick in the ribs or a pat on the head.
Nevertheless it is hardly fair
To risk your heart for a dog to tear.

When the fourteen years which Nature permits
Are closing in asthma, or tumour, or fits,
And the vet's unspoken prescription runs
To lethal chambers or loaded guns,
Then you will find – it's your own affair,
But … you've given your heart to a dog to tear.

When the body that lived at your single will,
When the whimper of welcome is stilled (how still!),
When the spirit that answered your every mood
Is gone – wherever it goes – for good,
You will discover how much you care,
And will give your heart to a dog to tear!

We've sorrow enough in the natural way,
When it comes to burying Christian clay.
Our loves are not given, but only lent,
At compound interest of cent per cent.
Though it is not always the case, I believe,
That the longer we've kept 'em, the more do we grieve:
For, when debts are payable, right or wrong,
A short-term loan is as bad as a long –
So why in Heaven (before we are there!)
Should we give our hearts to a dog to tear?

Patrick Chalmers (1872–1942)

To a Terrier

Crib, on your grave beneath the chestnut boughs
To-day no fragrance falls, nor summer air,
Only a master's love who laid you there
Perchance may warm the earth 'neath which you drowse
In dreams from which no dinner-gong may rouse,
Unwakeable, though close the rat may dare,
Deaf, though the rabbit thump in playful scare,
Silent, though twenty tabbies pay their vows.
And yet, mayhap, some night when shadows pass,
And from the fir the brown owl hoots on high,
Then, should one whistle 'neath a favouring star,
Your small white shade shall patter o'er the grass,
Questing for him you lov'd, o' days gone by,
Ere Death, the Dog-Thief, carried you afar.

Index of Authors

List of Illustrations

All images are from the collections of the British Library unless otherwise stated.

p. 2 Dogs bear baiting, 1521, from *The Varieties of Dogs, as they are found in old sculptures, pictures, engravings, and books* by Philibert Charles Berjeau, 1863 (7294.dd.6)

p. 8 Cocker Spaniel, from *A Book of Dogs* by W.R. Stark, 1921 (LB.31.b.14084)

p. 12 Illustration by Janet and Anne Grahame-Johnstone, from *The Hundred and One Dalmatians* by Dodie Smith, 1956 (17925.eee.110)

p. 15 'Japanese Dogs', illustration from *The Queen*, 19 October 1889

p. 16 Detail from the title page of *The Booke of Faulconrie or Hauking for the onely delight and pleasure of all Noblemen & Gentlemen* by George Turberville, 1575 (G.2372.(1))

p. 18 Greyhound, from *Historia Animalum* by Conrad Gesner, 1551–87 (460.c.1-3)

p. 24 Border illumination by Giovanni Pietro Birago from *Sforza Hours, c.* 1490–94 (Add. MS 34294, vol.ii, f. 122v)

pp. 26–27 Dachshund, from *Oliver Herford's Animal Book, with pictures by the author,* 1906 (12813.y.5)

p. 28 Illustration by Cecil Aldin from *A Dog Day; or, The Angel in the House* by Walter Emanuel, 1902 (12812.dd.16)

p. 33 'Mickey', from *Dogs of Character* written and illustrated by Cecil Aldin, 1927 (7295.i.32)

p. 35 The hunter and his dogs, from *The Costume of Yorkshire* by George Walker, 1885 (1756.c.7)

p. 38 Illustration by Cecil Aldin from *A Dog Day; or, The Angel in the House* by Walter Emanuel, 1902 (12812.dd.16)

p. 40 'Corrie', a Scotch terrier with a dead rat lying at its feet, watercolour, Nepalese school, *c.* 1862 (Add.Or.2614)

p. 44 Advertisement for Elliman's Embrocation, from *The Queen*, 14 November 1914

p. 51 'In the woods side by side White Fang ran with Collie', illustration by Charles Livingstone Bull, from *White Fang* by Jack London, 1906 (YD.2015.a.258)

p. 54 Miniature of the dog of Antioch that attacked the murderer of its master, from a Bestiary, 2nd or 3rd quarter of the 13th century (Sloane MS 3544, f. 13v)

p. 61 Woodcut by Thomas Bewick, from *Bewick's Woodcuts* by Thomas Hugo, 1870

p. 65 'Ulysses and his dog', illustration by John Flaxman from *The Odyssey of Homer* translated by Alexander Pope, 1866 (11316.aa.7)

p. 76 Illustration specimen for *Good Words for 1871* as advertised in *The Bookseller* 12 December 1871 (LOU.LD65)

p. 81 'He stopped, raced back, and came up to ask my will', illustration by Marguerite Kimsie to *Garm: A Hostage* from *Collected Dog Stories* by Rudyard Kipling, 1934 (12602.r.27)

p. 90 'When is this going to end?', illustration by Marguerite Kimsie to *Garm: A Hostage* from *Collected Dog Stories* by Rudyard Kipling, 1934 (12602.r.27)

p. 95 Illustration from back cover of *A Book of Dogs* by W. R. Stark, 1921 (LB.31.b.14084)

p. 96 'The wanderer sprang towards his master with delight', illustration from *Great Deeds of the Great War* by Donald Alexander Mackenzie, 1916 (1873.b.7)

p. 100 Miniature of a dog and his dead master from a theological miscellany, 2nd or 3rd quarter of the 13th century (Harley MS 3244, f. 45)

p. 103 Illustration of 'Pets in War' from *Great Deeds of the Great War* by Donald Alexander Mackenzie, 1916 (1873.b.7)

p. 104 *The Hound of the Baskervilles*, illustration by Sidney Paget from the original publication in *The Strand*, 1902 (P.P.6004.glk)

p. 106 'A horseman came on full gallop', illustration by Edmund H. Garrett from *Jane Eyre* by Charlotte Bronte, 1897 (12624.d.15)

p. 109 Bill Sykes and Bull's Eye, illustration by Fred Barnard from *Oliver Twist* by Charles Dickens, 1871 (12603.h.13)

p. 111 The Hound of the Baskervilles, illustration by Sidney Paget from the original publication in *The Strand*, 1902 (P.P.6004.glk)

p. 120 Illustration from *A Child's Primer of Natural History* by Oliver Herford, 1900 (12809.q.21)

p. 133 Dora, illustration by Fred Barnard from *David Copperfield* by Charles Dickens, 1871 (C.194.b.116)

p. 134 Woodcut by Thomas Bewick from *A General History of Quadrupeds* by R. Beilby, 1804 (1256.e.18)

p. 135 Frontispiece to *Flush: A Biography of Elizabeth Barrett Browning's Cocker Spaniel* by Virginia Woolf, 1933 (07294.h.10)

p. 137 Illustration by Marguerite Kimsie from *Greyfriars Bobby* by Eleanor Atkinson, 1929 (012601.l.7)

p. 144 Illustration by Thomas Cranc from *At Home* by J. G. Sowerby, 1881 (12805.k.41)

p. 150 Drawing by G. L. Stampa from *Supplication of the Black Aberdeen* by Rudyard Kipling, 1929 (File 487)

p. 154 Illustration by Marguerite Kimsie from *Collected Dog Stories* by Rudyard Kipling, 1934 (File 421)

For Bess

First published in 2015 by
The British Library
96 Euston Road
London NW1 2DB

Ray Bradbury: 'The Emissary' reprinted by permission of Abner Stein.
Frances Cornford: 'A Child's Dream' reprinted by permission of the Estate of
Frances Cornford. **Geoffrey Dearmer:** 'The Turkish Trench Dog' reprinted by
permission of the Estate of Geoffrey Dearmer. **Eleanor Farjeon:** 'Dog' from
Silver Sand and Snow published by Michael Joseph, reprinted by permission of
David Higham Associates. **Dodie Smith:** extract from *The Hundred and One
Dalmatians* copyright © 1956 Dodie Smith, with kind permission of Laurence
Fitch Ltd. **Dorothy Margaret Stuart:** 'King George's Dalmatian AD 1822'
© Dorothy Margaret Stuart. Every effort has been made to trace copyright
holders and to obtain their permission for the use of copyright material. The
publisher apologises for any errors or omissions and would be grateful if
notified of any corrections that should be incorporated in reprints or future
editions of this book.

Illustrations copyright © 2015 The British Library Board

Cataloguing in Publication Data
A catalogue record for this book is available
from the British Library

ISBN 978 0 7123 5776 0

Designed by Briony Hartley, Goldust Design
Cover by Rawshock Design
Printed in Malta by Gutenberg Press